MW00711433

ANCHORED
IN
ILLUSION

ANCHORED
IN
ILLUSION

BETH RENGEL

Published in the United States of America

ISBN: 978-1-68118-642-9
1. Biography & Autobiography / General
2. Biography & Autobiography / Women
16.08.22

This book is dedicated to my mother, Serena, and my daughter, Ana, who have been my bookends, and to my sister, Elaine, who is the page turner.

CONTENTS

FOREWORD

It was over a decade ago when I received a call at my office requesting an appointment for a meeting with Beth Rengel. That simple phone call created a flood of memories and emotions in my mind.

I had grown up in Tulsa, Oklahoma, and had enjoyed a typical Midwestern upbringing until, as a teenager, I was diagnosed with a condition that would cause me to lose my sight. My plans of being a professional athlete were shattered, along with any other ideas I had ever had about what I might do with my life. Trying to visualize myself as a blind person fitting in anywhere just didn't seem to work.

At that same time in Tulsa, there were billboards, commercials, and media announcements about a new broadcaster coming to town named Beth Rengel. As a teenager who still had my sight at that time, the photos and video images of Beth Rengel immediately informed me and everyone else in town that this was not going to be your typical, gray-haired, middle-aged guy in a business suit delivering the news each night. Beth Rengel, through some trials and tribulations, proved to her colleagues and everyone at home watching her on television that she was much more than a pretty face.

In the ensuing decades, Beth has had a world of experiences, dealt with triumph and tragedy and, through it all, has become a person that you will enjoy getting to know within the pages of this book.

That first meeting with Beth Rengel in my office created a bond between Beth and me that has made us colleagues and friends. The book you are reading now has been in the making for a decade, and the stories and experiences that make up this book are the products of a rich and full lifetime.

As an author of twenty-seven books and as someone who has had six of his novels turned into movies, I am always looking for a great story. As a best-selling fiction writer, I pride myself on creating fascinating characters and putting them in the middle of compelling stories. But on my best day, I could not have created a fictitious character as powerful, fascinating, and diverse as the real-life Beth Rengel you are preparing to meet.

As you read Beth's story and experience her life, please do as I have done while getting to know Beth and use her experiences and perspective to create a context that will allow you to anchor your own priorities while stretching your potential beyond the apparent impossibilities.

—Jim Stovall

INTRODUCTION

My life hasn't turned out the way I planned it. Maybe no one's life does. We buy into the illusions we face every day—illusions of the happy family, the flawless body, the picture-perfect marriage, the thriving career. But then we hit that inevitable brick wall of reality, and those illusions shatter. And then what? When that curveball comes straight at you, the question is: do you duck, swerve to the side, or stand firmly and try to catch it?

Life has thrown me some curveballs. For a long time, I got caught up in the illusions, and over and over again, I was devastated to discover that the reality—the truth about my family, my community, my career, my society, even myself—wasn't compatible with those illusions and never would be.

Beauty and brains, success and failure, career and family, marriage and divorce—these are all two sides of the same coin. Even though we human beings like to deny it, in the end, there is no avoiding the reality. You flip the coin, and the illusion is no more: Heads, you win. Tails, you lose. That's the terrible, beautiful reality of life, and it's nothing if not an adventure.

Throughout my own journey, I have learned that the nature of human beings is to resist going behind the illusion, to resist change. The irony is, though, that the very changes that can bring us down can build us back up if we choose. I am still in the process of putting down the burden of pretense and sharing what I think truly matters, but I've come to believe that *failure itself is an illusion*, one that covers up the next success—just a correction in course that can redirect us to what really matters in life. And though sometimes we will fail, only by seeking whatever is beyond the illusions can we find true purpose. We have to take risks to live by what's truly important.

This book is about taking risks, being knocked down, and getting back up. It's about learning not to judge others and learning to find your voice. After all, there is a light to be found inside all of us, and we each have a voice that yearns to be heard.

After much searching and confusion and discovery—and, yes, a great deal of risk—I have finally found my own light, my own voice. I have found some semblance of inner peace.

This book is not intended to hurt anyone, and I'm sure there are many versions of what happened where my life intersected with others' lives. What you are about to read is just my experience. It's how I lived it and how I remember it. I am like every woman who has tried to be a good daughter, wife, mother, and career woman—a survivor of our times. You may not understand where I'm coming from or see eye to eye with me. On the other hand, you may see a bit of yourself in my experiences.

As I've said, in my life, I've endured plenty of curveballs, roundabout paths to the measure of success and happiness that I have reached today. Some of these were divine intervention, others were a result of decisions I made, and still others were just plain cockeyed by default. One of the most formative of these experiences was the most embarrassing moment in my professional career as an evening newscaster, an event that caused me a lot of public pain and problems—and more than a little humiliation. But as the tears dried, I learned something about myself: the word *quit* is not in my vocabulary.

1

My Most Embarrassing Moment

> Life is a series of adjustments…Get ready!
>
> —Beth Rengel

Oh my gosh. I said what? a little voice screamed inside my head. My heart was in my throat.

What have I done? I thought, closing my eyes for a moment as the awful realization washed over me. It had been an accident, a slip-up. I hadn't meant to say it aloud. No one should have heard. The station was technically off the air, but we weren't. I hadn't muttered those words only to myself. My microphone was live, and my words had just gone out *over the air,* on live TV.

And what I had said was not pretty.

A Slip of the Tongue

What have I done?

I knew it was bad, but I had no idea of the firestorm that would come from that slip of the tongue.

It was February 1980. It had been a long winter, but it was about to get even colder for me. I was the female coanchor, doing the one-hour newscast at 5:00 p.m.—a prime slot—and it wasn't going well. We didn't wear double mikes the way newscasters do now as backup, a delay in case something goes wrong during a live broadcast.

During that night's 5:00 p.m. news, for the first half hour, the people living in and around Tulsa, Oklahoma, must have noticed that Beth Rengel hadn't said a single word. There I sat, between anchorman Bob Hower and sportscaster Chris Lincoln, silent as the grave.

Why the silence? It hadn't started out that way at the top of the hour. Bob had led, as always, and I had launched in with a bright, "Good evening, I'm Beth Rengel..." But that's as far as I got, because after my introduction, my microphone went dead.

My frustration had mounted. Even thinking about it now, I imagine myself as one of those little bobbleheads you see on a car's dashboard or back window, nodding its head with a fake grin on its face. I felt like an idiot, looking back and forth from the newscaster to the sportscaster and back to the newscaster, a forced smile covering my growing irritation and embarrassment. If you've never been on live TV, unable to say a word and yet unable to get off the camera, you have no idea how long half an hour actually is—it's *forever*.

Finally, Bob tossed to Don Woods, the weatherman. Steve Van Dyne, the audio man, came running out of the control room to change out my microphone.

"Test, test...It's working!" he announced.

Thank goodness, I thought. *Here's my chance to redeem myself!* The viewers hadn't known why I was sitting there in silence, but now I could explain, put the audio difficulties behind me, and go on with my job.

Moving on from weather, Bob Hower began reading his next story, but now, incredibly, his mike went out too!

My face flushed as I felt the chaos mounting in the studio.

"Take the story!" the producer was screaming in my ear. "Bob's mike isn't working! Take the story!"

No one else got that message at first, but finally the camera went to me.

"We are so sorry for our audio difficulties this evening," I began, but as I took my next breath, every monitor in the studio went black. I knew what that meant—every newscaster does. We were technically off the air.

Now what? I groaned inwardly. I couldn't believe it! The frustration had built up to the breaking point. I muttered to myself, "Goddamn it, what's going on?"

Those five words would come back to haunt me for a long time.

We went to a commercial break, but it was too late. The news director, George Stewart, came flying into the studio like Tom Cruise in *Risky Business*, sliding into the living room in his white socks. He was practically shrieking, "That went out over the air! Beth, your mike was *live*! You just cursed over the air."

Though the monitors had all gone black, one mike had still been open—mine. I was mortified. I'd grown up in the Southern Baptist church, and I never cursed—well, until that night. I had always been a good girl, trained to say what I was supposed to say and not say what I wasn't. That night, though, everyone tuning in to the evening news heard my calm demeanor crack. Viewers at home saw a black screen, but they heard my faint, muttering voice loud and clear. That dooming comment was live on the air. Perhaps today, or even back then in some other parts of the country, those five words wouldn't be quite as much of a shock to the people at home in the living room and at the dinner table, but in Tulsa in 1980, it was a big deal. After all, this was the Bible Belt, and Tulsa was the buckle.

Even today, Tulsa is very conservative, and back then it was much more so. Already, men and women, especially women, would call in to criticize me for the smallest thing: my hair, my earrings, how I read a story. Well, there was no possibility that they would overlook this! The irony was staggering: after years as a woman striving to be taken seriously, finally, at the worst possible moment, I would be judged not on how I looked, but entirely on what I'd said.

While on commercial break, I immediately turned to Bob, the stabilizing presence at the news desk.

"What do I do?" I asked frantically. I wanted to apologize on the air right then and there. I wanted to fix it.

"Beth," Bob said calmly, unflappable, "just ignore it."

Ignore it? I thought. *That can't be right.* But I trusted Bob, the veteran broadcaster. Surely, he knew what was best in this situation.

Back from commercial, we wrapped up the broadcast with no further complications. Later, we did the 10:00 p.m. newscast without a hitch, but I surely knew that wasn't the end of it. What would happen? Was my career in jeopardy? I didn't know, but I felt certain there would be repercussions.

Feeling wrung out and desperate, I headed home. The waiting was unbearable. I didn't sleep a wink all that agonizing night. The next morning, I got a call from my news director, George.

"Beth," he began, sounding sad on the other end of the line, "don't come in today. You're off the air...for now."

I closed my eyes and tried to catch my breath. "For how long?" I choked out.

"I don't know," he replied. "It's Mr. Leake's decision, and it's indefinite for now."

I was utterly in shock. The station owner, James Leake, had ordered me not to come in. Did that mean the repercussions were going to be even more serious than I'd feared?

Indeed, the fallout was immediate, and it was huge. My fate hung in the balance for weeks. I didn't know what the future would hold, but I was determined I would be the one to shape it. I wasn't going to sit back and let anyone, not even the TV station owner, determine my future for me. I had three choices: give up, give in, or get back up!

Being knocked down is hard. I've experienced it many times in many ways, though my on-air gaffe in Tulsa was the most publicly humiliating. But one of the crucial lessons life has taught me is that it's not what happens to us that's significant—it's *how we react* to what happens to us. The way I was raised taught me the importance of getting back up when you've taken a fall, big or small. Fear of failure can paralyze us. It can leave us curled up on the kitchen floor—and believe me, I've been there. We can just stay there, beaten, or we can push through that fear and go on to take the risk again, to welcome success and failure alike as just more lessons from life.

Life has proven to me that we must walk through the illusion of our fears and the illusion of perfection. Nobody is perfect, so why should we fear failure? We must take risks, or we'll never know what we might be capable of.

Was my most publicly embarrassing moment truly a failure, or was it just a potential success masquerading as a setback? If we live in a life of illusions, perhaps the greatest illusion of all is failure.

2

The Illusion of the Perfect Childhood as a Texan

The only thing real about your past is the love you gave and the love you received. All else was illusion that can now be let go.

—Marianne Williamson,
spiritual teacher and author

I grew up poor, though I didn't really know it at the time. As I got older, I made up for it. I made sure I wouldn't have to be poor forever, slowly but surely building a life with all the available comforts. Still, I never stopped trying to recapture a perfect childhood that never was. In my mind, there was always a white picket fence out there somewhere, waiting for me and my own family someday.

At the Kitchen Table

I came from South Texas and grew up in the 1950s as Mae Beth Cormany. Those days were so much simpler and slower, before technology brought the fast-paced world directly into America's homes. Childhood was both a little more precarious and a little more carefree back then. Church and Sunday school were a big part of life for my sister and me. Every night, we would sit down as a family and eat supper together. My father was a used car salesman, and my mother stayed at home to cook, clean, and sew. My sister was six years older and wanted very little to do with her bratty younger sister.

I remember when we got our first television, a large square box that entered our living room and our lives, portraying suburban perfection to millions of Americans. I'm not saying it was *Ozzie and Harriet* at my house—far from it—but the illusion of the happy family, the happy childhood, is what I bought into. It started a rock slide of perfection, a pattern built on the flawed fantasy of a flawless life. Ever since, I have strived to achieve every happy illusion out there.

Writing about the world around me was another pattern that came early. This was a time when the Beatles first landed on American soil, a time when our country was torn by racial segregation. I started covering the news in the seventh grade, though I didn't know then that I was doing so. My very first memory of writing is documenting the assassination of President John F. Kennedy in my turquoise diary. Even then, I was hungry to write, though I've never been quite sure what inspired that hunger. But my memories betray the unstable collective illusion of life in those days: I remember jumping rope on the school playground one day and the next day hiding under my school desk during nuclear bomb drills.

Some things that happen as a child, you never forget. For me, one of those is the feeling of summer nights in South Texas. In my memories, it was hot—*always* hot. My family lived in a few rental houses over the years: in Corpus Christie, in Brownsville, and in McAllen, where the mosquito problem was almost insufferable. My sister, Elaine, and I had our own rooms, but I was sure my window had more holes in its screen. During summer, especially, I faced a nightly decision: sleep with a sheet over me and stifle in the heat or throw off the sheet and wake up to mosquito bites in the morning. Sleeping with the window closed was not an option. Air-conditioning was another astounding piece of technology, especially for those of us living at the very bottom tip of the country, where America meets Mexico over the Rio Grande. My parents, at the end of the hall, had a window unit, but their door stayed closed at night.

My father, David, was forced to quit high school during his junior year. His father needed him to help work in the bottling company—a Coca-Cola franchise. Dad was the youngest of eight children, and he did what he was told. He brought my sister and me up the same way—to mind our elders, work hard, and be tough.

My father was a tall, handsome man, blond and blue-eyed. When he was happy, everyone was happy, but when he wasn't, that illusion of our happy family could disintegrate in a heartbeat. I think deep down he was an angry, dissatisfied man. Surely, he'd had dreams once, like all of us, and those dreams were squelched, but never, and I mean *never*, would he talk about what those lost dreams were. I don't think he was capable of sharing like that, particularly as a man of his generation.

I often return to a recurring memory of my dad. He always appears the same in these memories, wearing a sleeveless white T-shirt and sitting under a light at the kitchen table, rolling his own cigarettes. I am sitting beside him, holding out the next sheer white paper as he reaches for it. My dad wordlessly takes the paper, places it in the empty spot left by the last one, pours a little tobacco across it, carefully rolls it, and licks one side of the paper till it sticks. It's an image that is, to me, the essence of my father.

My dad could be rather rough on the outside, so it always surprised me when I'd walk past his room and see him sitting on the edge of the bed, watching *Little House on the Prairie* or *The Waltons* and crying silent tears. Perhaps many of us have that need for the heartfelt stories those TV shows portrayed. The American frontier days and the Great Depression years were full of hard times, but in these shows, the family members' love for one another was unstoppable. Every day ended with an affirmation: "Good night, John Boy." It was easy to buy into that illusion.

My mother, Serena, was a small, slim, dark-haired lady with beautiful, fair features. I knew my mother and father loved each other, even though Mom cried a lot. My dad wasn't always easy to live with, and my mom worried about money. She was an amazing cook and homemaker who made us eat liver once a week. She also made all our clothes. I didn't have a store-bought outfit until I was seventeen. In elementary school, a group of girls would make fun of my homemade clothes, snickering and bullying me until I wanted to cry. Often, I pretended to be sick so I could stay home from school, but we couldn't afford a new wardrobe at the start of every school year, so hand-me-downs and homemade outfits were what my sister and I wore.

Of course, I made up for all that when I got into beauty pageants and later the news industry, buying designer clothes to match my fake red fingernails. But when I remember my childhood, most of the time, I see my mother in front of the sewing machine. In those days, being a wife and mother was just what a good girl grew up expecting to do.

During the Christmas holidays, though, Mom left home each day to work at the S&H Green Stamp Store in order to buy gifts for us and our relatives. I think it was the first time she showed any independence from my father. It was for the good of the family, so that made it okay in her mind.

To this day, I can remember licking the stamps and putting them in these little books after we bought groceries. We would count how many books we had and dream about the things we could buy with them. We turned in a bunch of stamp books one time for a shiny new toaster. It wasn't much, but it felt as though we were getting those things free.

One late afternoon when we lived in Brownsville, my mother was at the kitchen sink, doing dishes, and suddenly whirled around, gathering my sister and me and pulling us to the floor. She had seen something out the window. The three of us huddled under that same kitchen table where my father had rolled hundreds of cigarettes. What was it that Mom saw? A Sears and Roebuck truck pulling into the driveway to repossess our sofa.

The knocks on the back door seemed deafening. I felt safe hunkering down from the "bad guys" with my mother protecting us, but the look in her eyes made an enduring impression on me. I knew immediately that I never wanted to see that look of fear or feel that shame again. I swore then, at age six, that I would never be in my mother's situation. Maybe that's when I started dreaming of those white picket fences.

Down a Country Road

When I was a kid, our idea of a vacation was to spend the night in a motel and go swimming in a pool surrounded by a chain-link fence. We would drive up to San Antonio, sometimes in a car with no air-conditioning, to stay at the Modern Motel while my dad bid on cars at an auction. It might have been just a cut-rate business trip for Dad, but we didn't care. For us, it was true luxury. Our room had two beds and an *air conditioner*. When our "summer vacation" was over, we would caravan back home, with Mom driving our car and Dad driving one car he had bought while towing another.

But the best vacations were to my grandmother's house. Each year on Christmas Eve, at the crack of dawn, my family would load into the station wagon and head for Valley Mills, Texas (population: 1,000), nestled between Waco and Clifton. Usually, my sister and I were still in our pajamas, but we didn't need to bundle up—even in the dead of winter, temperatures rarely got cooler than the eighties. The car was filled to the brim with Christmas presents, and my sister and I would push them aside as we crawled into the back and returned to sleep on an old handmade quilt.

And so our journey would begin. My parents ate doughnuts to fuel them for the eight-hour jaunt north. As the long drive progressed, I could tell we were getting closer to our destination because the skies got lighter, the sun got higher, and the air got cooler. By midafternoon, my sister and I would recognize that we were getting near the turnoff. Then it would happen—that moment I'd been waiting for all year long. Dad would slow the car down and pull off the smooth black highway onto an old country road.

It seemed as though we traveled far off into the countryside along that narrow winding gravel road, away from the fast-paced world and the troubles of home. My dad drove slowly, and I stuck my head out of the back window, watching the gravel kick up dust behind us to announce our grand entrance. I relished the feel of the cold wind brushing my long hair off my face. I loved that long dirt road and the smell of the cedar trees that lined it. I could taste the dirt, too, and feel it in my eyes, but I didn't care. I knew where we were going.

This house was a happy house. It was a big white house with a white picket fence around it and my grandmother's garden under the sweet scent of the mimosa tree. As we drew near the end of that long country road, I could see the mountain we'd climb later to chop down a scrub cedar for our Christmas tree. I could already taste the delicious food my grandmother was cooking in her yellow kitchen wafting over the flying dust and ancient cedars: roasted ham and turkey, fluffy buttered rolls, apple pie.

My grandparents' old dog, Jeff, would come up to greet our car. My dad would honk the horn and yell, "We're here!" out the car window, triggering the flood of loving relatives who would pour out the front door. But like a sixth sense, my grandmother would be out the side door already, wearing her handmade apron but all dressed up underneath, scooping us up in big hugs that smelled of homemade turkey dressing.

The sights, the smells—they were perfection to me, an ideal I've tried to recapture throughout my life.

Years later, after my grandparents were gone, I revisited Valley Mills, wanting to relive those wonderful moments that helped shape my life, but turning off the highway, I noticed something was very wrong. The house was vacant now, run-down, and much smaller than I remembered. The mountain had been reduced to a hill, and that long country road was in fact merely a gravel driveway.

It made me mad and sad. The little girl in me wanted that back. Was it all a dream? I cannot ever live those happy moments again. Were they even real? Well, yes, it was all real, yet it was also an illusion, the best kind of illusion we can have—a child's image of happiness that we hold on to like a warm blanket in this cold, harsh world. That old house with the white picket fence was more than just a house beside a hill in northern Texas. The long road to get there represented the anticipation of being surrounded by family and love. The distance we drove was nothing compared with the journey of memories I've cherished and revisited for decades.

This image of the house and all it embodied for me formed a concept of happiness that cut two ways. As I grew up, it taught me that life is all about the long journey that brings us across bumps, through dust, and finally beneath sweet-smelling cedars to our destination. My happy memories ultimately shaped my approach to life and gave me something to strive for. But coming face to face with the truth, I was startled to realize that my idea of happiness had been built on a child's fantasy.

Through the eyes of an adult, our dreams of childhood are bigger than reality, and that's okay—it's the innocence. I guess that's the way it's supposed to be. Later in our years, we might become jaded and world-weary. I know I have been. We realize that true joy can be found at a motel pool on a hot Texas day, and that even a three-thousand-square-foot home may be inhabited by unhappy people. Perhaps that's where their illusion drove them, before it proved to be just that: an empty illusion.

A Favorite Picture...or Not?

Maybe we need illusions in our lives, and sometimes we'll do anything to create or recreate that perfect—whatever. We'll buy what we think we have to buy, celebrate the way we're expected to celebrate, dress for the success we're seeking, and smile and laugh as if it's all going to last—as if that "Kodak moment" were real.

I have a photograph of my parents that sums up their relationship and the circumstances of my childhood, though it was taken many years later at my house during the Christmas holidays with my own daughter. It's one of my favorite pictures, I think. My mother and father are hugging and smiling—the happy couple, David and Serena Cormany of Wichita Falls, Texas. They were both very proud of being from Texas, so I put the picture in a bronze-colored frame covered with little cowboy hats, boots, and longhorn cattle on it. The grins on both of their faces—pure, joyful—call up many of my own childhood memories of the holidays, both good and bad. My mom is wearing red, as always, for the holiday. My dad is wearing a navy striped velour sweater, his right arm draped protectively around my mother's shoulders. Both are looking directly into the camera as if to dare you *not* to see how happy they are in this particular moment.

Sometime later that day, tempers probably flared as they always did during the holidays. Most of the time, it was the result of my dad's drinking—vodka, maybe, or wine. The mood of the gathering would shift as he became argumentative. We all knew it was the booze. He would try to have fun and enjoy the holiday, but invariably he would get his feelings hurt and then get in the car and leave.

Decades later, I don't remember exactly how the rest of the day went, but I savor the moment that photograph portrays—that illusion of a happy family. Today, I keep that framed photograph of my parents in my den. To the casual observer, it's the epitome of perfect grandparents and an idealistic holiday, but I know the truth behind the illusion.

The dictionary definition tells us that an illusion is "something that deceives by producing a false or misleading impression of reality." Family pictures—today more than ever, with Instagram and Facebook portraying perfection in so many families—are the quintessential illusion, a moment we capture and then present as our own personal reality. I choose to believe some of these wonderful illusions do become reality. When we hold out ideal images of our life or the things we think will make us happy, we find ourselves striving to reach those goals—to be a teacher, a doctor, a philanthropist, or even just a good parent. Illusions can be a good thing, unless you're clutching them for the wrong reasons and they end up strangling you.

I'm talking now about our hands reaching out to grasp the illusions all around us: money, status, stuff. It's everywhere. Pick up a magazine, watch a TV commercial, get on the Internet, see a roadside billboard, listen to the radio—you'll be convinced that all you need to do is buy this or achieve that, and everything will be okay. "I would be happy if only I had…" This is nothing new to human nature, but never has it been so prevalent. Illusions dominate career, marriage, religion, politics, the aging process, even our childhood memories. They are out there for the taking, and we pick the ripest ones and gobble them up like low-hanging fruit.

Some of the most detrimental illusions, though, are the ones we create about ourselves. We trick ourselves into believing we're on the right road, doing the right thing, being the person we're supposed to be—until something happens to wake us up, a breakdown in that make-believe journey. Then we see the mirage for what it is—someone else's idea of perfection—and we have to rebuild our idea of ourselves all over again. Sometimes we do that over and over in life. When you are pursuing someone else's illusion, how will you ever fulfill your own dreams?

As a child, I thought I wanted to be an architect. I was fascinated with homes and their layout. I would sit on the floor with a pencil and tablet and recreate house plans. Mom would bring home *Better Homes and Gardens* magazine, and I loved looking at the perfect houses on those colorful pages and could doodle for hours. I think now that, rather than the structure of a house, in my mind I was forever building the illusion of a happy home, a happy family.

Of course, I did not go on to become an architect. That was a man's profession. I was content watching my mom be a good wife and mother, presuming I would follow in her footsteps. I didn't know that my experiences and innocence would lead me on an unsustainable search for fulfillment through perfection. I didn't know I would forever be seeking white picket fences, long country roads, and quiet moments at the kitchen table.

No matter how things develop, it's what's in our hearts that carries us through each day.

In my heart, the memories of childhood are strong, so I focus on the truth at the core of my happy childhood illusions. It's been a long journey, a struggle through illusion after illusion, and that journey continues. According to *A Course in Miracles* by clinical psychologist Helen Schucman, "The past is over. It can touch me not." Despite all else, and above all else, the love of my family is the one real thing I can take away from my childhood, and it's the one true thing from childhood that matters now.

3

The Roller Coaster Pageant Ride

You must make a choice to take a chance,
or you will never change.

—Zig Ziglar, motivational speaker

If there is one pivotal moment that marks the end of my not-so-perfect childhood, it's the morning my father sat me down and said, "Mae Beth, you're graduating high school this year. Now you have three choices: get a job, get married, or get a scholarship."

These were not promising options. I wasn't anywhere near marriage. I had no job prospects or serious thoughts on what sort of work I might pursue. No colleges were offering scholarships to a solid but average student. As my father's words sank in, I started to panic. I didn't know what I was going to do with my life.

It was the spring of 1969. I was a senior in high school in Wichita Falls, Texas. My older sister had set the bar high, earning a four-year scholarship to North Texas State University in Denton, Texas, because of her amazing voice and then going on to study in New York. She had become a well-known lyric opera singer in Europe. That was a hard act to follow, but I had no choice. It was time to do, to try, and to risk failure.

Three Clichés That Changed My Life

I walked home from school that hot afternoon wondering what my future would hold. As I opened the screen door, a flier fell out. It was a black-and-white photo, a head shot of a brunette with a very tall beehive hairdo. As I recall, her name was Olive Meadows. How pretty is that? And so was she—beautiful, in fact. It was her face that first drew me in, and only afterward did I notice that the flier proclaimed, "You Could Be Miss Astros!"

The Miss Astros Contest was an annual promotion for Houston's Major League Baseball team. Local radio stations held contests to select their candidates for the title. There was no talent involved. The contestants—from Texas, Louisiana, Oklahoma, Arkansas, and New Mexico—were judged strictly on looks and the interview, which purported to reveal their charm, intelligence, and personality. The flier revealed that the prizes were enormous: a four-year college scholarship (wow!), a brand-new Toyota, a Rolex watch, a wardrobe, a trip for two to Puerto Vallarta, *and* Samsonite luggage! And the winner would be featured at many public and social functions during the year.

According to my perception of myself, I was cute and friendly. Sure, I'd been voted cheerleader each year, through two years of middle school and four years of high school, but a pageant?

I took one look at the flier, then stepped into the kitchen and tossed it into the trash can.

My mom was home, in the kitchen as usual. It was a Tuesday, so she was making chocolate chip cookies. "Now wait a minute. What is that?" she asked, reaching into the garbage. Her hand, weathered by years of yard work and hot dishwater, retrieved the flier and held it out to me.

I shook my head no. "It's just a pageant thing," I replied. "I can't do that. I don't do that."

"All you have to do is enter the radio contest," Mom countered.

I looked at her as though she'd lost her marbles. "Mom, I'm not a pageant person."

Cue the infamous trio of clichés.

"You know what I always say, Mae Beth: you'll never know unless you try. Your grandmother always said, 'You don't regret the things you do but the things you don't do.' And as far as your dad, 'Well, hell, if you fail, it's better than a kick in the ass.' Do you want to live the rest of your life wondering what might have been?"

That made me mad, because she was right. I left the kitchen with a huge question in my heart and head: what if? Opportunities weren't exactly knocking on my door, and yet one of the three options from my father's list, a scholarship, had dropped right into my lap. What did I have to lose? Those clichés haunted me. I mulled it over for days until I came to a decision: I knew I had to try.

I called the radio station to enter the contest. It didn't take long.

That was simple, I thought.

Two other girls entered the Wichita Falls contest, and the three of us talked with a radio disc jockey. To my shock, I won. I was chosen to represent the KWFT radio station for the Miss Astros Contest in Houston.

What have I done? I wondered, not for the last time. *I don't do this kind of thing!*

It was true: I had never entered a pageant of any kind, never even *thought* about entering one, but now there was no choice—I had to move onward and upward. So off to the fabric store we went, to pick out pink taffeta and a dress pattern, because naturally, Mom would be making my dress.

I can still see it now—an A-shape gown with a boatneck and three-quarters-length sleeves, a style that the model Twiggy had made popular in the late 1960s. We picked out some white cloth shoes from Kinney's, and my mom dyed them to match the exact color pink of the dress. Then, as creative as she was, she sewed pink flowers on the tip of each shoe. Now the hard part was finding a swimsuit for the other judging segment. At last, we found a black one-piece from Treasure City, the K-Mart of the day.

As time progressed and the contest drew near, I dreaded each day more than the one before. Then that fateful summer day arrived when the contestants would gather at the Astro World Hotel. My parents drove me to Houston…and left me there.

There were twenty-eight girls from five states. Many had false eyelashes. Some wore falls (today they're called extensions) and knew just how to walk in a swimsuit. These girls were *professionals.* At least, that's how it seemed to me.

As for me, I just wanted to go home. I didn't belong there. I had known that all along. Who was I trying to fool? These girls were true beauties, and they were totally out of my league. Throughout all the preliminaries and sit-down interviews, every move I made was being watched and silently judged, and I didn't like that feeling. It was intimidating to say the least.

The fear struck me most deeply at a luncheon with the five judges. We were at a beautiful restaurant with white tablecloths and fresh flowers on each table. It was the first time someone had ever watched me so closely as I ate. The main course was baked chicken, scalloped potatoes, a roll, and peas! Have you ever tried to eat peas with a fork? Well, it's not easy, especially under such scrutiny. I would dip my fork to the plate, pick up several peas, scoop the fork slowly toward my mouth—and watch in wide-eyed horror as each tiny green orb fell from its perch onto the table and then the floor. The first time, I was embarrassed. The second time, I was completely mortified.

Well, I'm sure I scored after that! I thought sarcastically. I felt ungainly and unworthy. *What am I doing here?*

All throughout lunch, I was watching the other girls—watching the other girls watch me—and watching the judges watch me and the other girls. We ate while they asked each of us questions. Now who on earth thought *that* would be a good idea? Needless to say, I was not enjoying my lunch at all.

Sunday arrived at last. Soon, the torture would end.

The setting was the Houston Astrodome during an extended pause between innings to announce the winner of the Miss Astros contest. All twenty-eight of us stood on the Astroturf diamond before thousands of baseball fans, awaiting our fate. I was beyond insecurity and beyond fear. I had successfully rendered myself numb. I just wanted to go home.

The announcer called the runner-ups' names over the loud-speaker. When I didn't hear my name, I thought, *Thank goodness, it's over. Now let's get out of here!* So I didn't even hear the next announcement: "And the winner is...Mae Beth Cormany from Wichita Falls!"

It took several girls shaking me and saying, "You won, you won!" before I finally snapped out of it. Then, of course, I covered my face and cried as I had seen so many pageant winners do. When I looked up, I saw a Toyota parked in one of the breezeways—my first car. And it was baby blue, to boot!

That event changed my life. That contest catapulted me toward entering the Miss Texas Pageant and later the Miss America Pageant, and it planted the seed of ambition that later would drive me to become a television news anchor. Becoming Miss Astros also started me down a slippery slope of relying on the illusion of beauty in my life and allowing others to characterize me as someone who relies on that illusion. But even so, it started a series of changes and challenges I never would have experienced or accomplished other-wise. Who knows what path my life might have taken without those three clichés about guts and grit? Those mottos balanced the flaws and frailties that come with striving to keep up so many illusions.

The illusion of beauty may be insidious, but so is the illusion of fear. We all need a push now and then. We need permission to try. We need to know that even if we don't win, the experience is not necessarily a failure. In fact, it can be our motivation to try again. After I was named Miss Astros, I realized that sometimes I might have to walk through that illusion of fear to reach my goals in life. We all do at one time or another.

The Ugly Swimsuit

One of my prizes for winning Miss Astros was a trip for two to a gorgeous Mexican beach resort in Puerto Vallarta, on the Pacific Ocean. I was only eighteen, so I offered the trip to my parents. My mother had never been on a plane before. They were so grateful, they decided to buy an airline ticket for me to join them.

I was beyond excited about the trip, but there was something bothering me: my swimsuit. It was an orange one-piece, several years old. I shared my concern with my mother, pleading, "Mom, I just want one thing: a two-piece swimsuit!"

She paused for a long moment and finally said, "Sure, honey. We'll just cut yours in half." And she did.

It was horrible. My mom was quite a seamstress, but she was no miracle worker. The top was halfway down my ribs, and the bottom looked like granny panties. It was not the look I was going for. I knew then that we weren't off to a good start.

Upon arriving in Mexico, we checked into the beautiful hotel, La Posada Vallarta, and walked into a wonderful white room over-looking the beach. French windows surrounded the room, with sheer white curtains that let the fresh, salty air blow inside. It was gorgeous, even if I had to share it with my parents.

But the first thing out of my father's mouth was "Goddamn it, where's the TV?"

We looked around the room again, as if we might have missed it the first time.

"You've got to be kidding!" my father ranted. "There's no TV?"

Well, there *was* no TV. This was a Mexican resort where celebrities like Elizabeth Taylor, Richard Burton, and director John Huston came to escape all that media blitz. So we spent our first day down on the beach—all day long. My dad, whose skin had never seen sunshine except from the forearms down, was beet red. My mother, who wore a black swimsuit from 1957 that came down over her thighs, drank the water and got sick. Our hotel room became an infirmary. My parents didn't go anywhere for days. And so there I sat.

My dad, who was very protective of his little girl, wouldn't let me out on my own to do anything. There was a young Mexican man, tall and handsome, who worked at the hotel and offered to show me around the town. My father's answer was a definite "No!" He was convinced I would meet a bunch of wild kids and fall in with the wrong crowd, especially since we were in a foreign country. Of course, meeting fun kids my age was exactly what I had in mind.

Some college kids were playing volleyball down on the beach, right in the surf, and all I wanted was to go down and meet them. But how could I get to know them? Surely, I couldn't just walk up and say, "Hey, guys…" Back then, I was too shy to speak—but not too shy to try something else.

When I finally got Dad to let me out of the room, I was bound and determined to figure out a way to meet those college kids, so I put on my ugly "two-piece" swimsuit and pulled out my secret weapon: the good old Wonderbra. This amazing undergarment has gone through a resurgence in recent decades, but back then, it was a simple though revolutionary concept: two pieces of shaped foam rubber that gave even the most flat-chested girl *instant cleavage*.

Suddenly, I felt like a woman.

I put my hair in pigtails and was all decked out, *Gidget Goes Hawaiian* style, trying to create an image that would get attention. I thought if I just walked by, surely they'd yell out, "Hey, wanna come play volleyball with us?"

So I headed down to the beach and started walking in the surf toward them. I was getting closer and closer, knee-deep in the ocean, and just as I'd reached them, I heard a loud noise. I looked up and saw a giant wave crashing onto the beach. Before I could do a thing, it knocked me down and carried me right up to where those college boys and girls were playing volleyball!

I was drenched, my plan wrecked—sand in my mouth, my eyes, and everywhere else. I was so embarrassed! But it got worse. As I picked myself up, I noticed that one of the foam pads was gone, and the other was hanging out of my swimsuit. I popped that one back in, and then I saw that the other pad had washed up onto the beach—right in front of these cute boys.

What could I do? My only hope was to get to it before they did, so I just walked over and quickly stomped on the missing foam pad. Then I reached down and picked it up, wrung out the water, and headed back to my parents' room with my head held high.

I felt so crushed, so defeated. I was a failure. That silly image of beauty I'd tried to create had been utterly destroyed—by a rogue wave, no less. I had gotten caught up in projecting the illusion of beauty and then been bowled over by the illusion of failure. In the end, it was not failure but just a setback. I eventually did meet those college kids, and my dad even let me hang out with them a little bit.

My attempt at saving face—the pretense of dignity that I'd somehow held on to as I beat my hasty retreat—was an illusion, too. The lesson I took from this was one I had learned in becoming Miss Astro and one I would use again and again in the future: sometimes you've got to fake it until you make it.

Headed to Miss Texas

When I got off the plane back in Texas, a member of the Wichita Falls Jaycees approached me at the airport and asked me to enter their local contest. The Junior Chamber is a national civic organization that emphasizes business development, training and leadership, and community service. In my hometown, the Jaycees ran the Miss Wichita Falls Pageant, a preliminary to the Miss Texas Pageant.

Miss Texas—this was a whole different ball game. The Miss Texas Pageant wasn't just a regional promotion for baseball fans— it was a live televised broadcast seen by the entire state of Texas. The winner would go on to...well, I couldn't even think about that right then.

Once again, as with the Miss Astros Contest, I hesitated. I still had a year to fulfill the duties of Miss Astros, which meant making appearances at Houston Astros games and promoting the baseball team. Besides, that whole experience of being judged and competing against such beautiful, poised women was way too hard, way too scary.

I told the Jaycee, "I can't do that. I don't have a talent."

He just smiled and said, "We can help you with that."

I had just returned from a free vacation at the beach. I had benefited from the Miss Astros scholarship and would soon be entering Midwestern University in Wichita Falls while proudly driving my first car—that pretty little baby blue Toyota. I was convinced that I had no real talent, but readily accepted that the Jaycees could help me apply some illusion of talent. Why not try my luck again?

I spent that year preparing for the Miss Texas pageant. I had to step up my game. Though I'd been singing in church and school choirs, now I had to raise it to the level of a bona fide talent. My sister, a recognized soprano, was the real talent. She sent me a musical rendition of a song from *My Fair Lady*. I learned it frontward and backward, and when I dressed up as a mop lady like Audrey Hepburn, singing "All I Want Is a Room Somewhere," I won the local preliminary. I was Miss Wichita Falls 1970.

Now on to the big show!

That week in July 1970—my first Miss Texas Pageant—I spent a lot of time sitting in my hotel room, anxiously looking out the window as if in search of an answer to that same question I'd had during the Miss Astros competition: *What in the world am I doing here?*

When a limo with a U-Haul trailer attached drove up to the hotel and stopped, it felt as if my world had stopped. I had only one thought in mind as I waited: *who in the heck will get out of that car?*

The driver slowly opened the limo's back door, and out stepped Phyllis George, Miss Dallas. Dressed in a white pantsuit, with long brown hair and a big Texas smile, she was the picture of elegance. And when the driver opened the back door of the trailer, two other men pulled out an elegant wardrobe to match—the longest rack of clothes I had ever seen.

My head slowly turned from the window toward my hotel room closet, where my one suitcase sat on the floor. *Oh my gosh*, I thought. *I'm in trouble.*

And I was right. That year was Phyllis George's second try at winning Miss Texas, and it worked. She was Miss Texas 1970. I came in third runner-up.

Surely, this was a sign. I simply wasn't smart enough, talented enough, or beautiful enough. In a way, it was a relief. Now I could finally retire from the pageant life and go back to being just plain Mae Beth Cormany.

But after my freshman year at Midwestern University, I transferred to Texas Christian University in Fort Worth, and the local Jaycees asked if I would represent *their* city in the Miss Fort Worth Pageant. I entered, won, and became Miss Fort Worth 1971. I would be returning to the Miss Texas Pageant after all.

The pageant bug had bitten.

Well, it goes without saying, those three clichés kicked in. It was all work every day until the next Miss Texas Pageant. I attended classes every day and worked out constantly. I read and did homework on the dorm floor while doing leg lifts. I did commercials on the side for spending money. I went home a few times a year to do television spots for a Wichita Falls bank. I trained with a voice teacher for the first time.

I loved any and all my classes that dealt with speech and phonetics, but I would read four chapters and be thinking about something else the whole time. I retained nothing. So I began to tape record each chapter and listen to it in my own voice. It worked.

My grades got even better, but I lost my Texas accent. All my life I had the typical, high-pitched Southern slang, and now it was gone—part of my identity erased in my search for perfection.

That year, sixty-eight beautiful and talented contestants came to Fort Worth from all over the huge state of Texas, each of them looking to win the title. A year had gone by since my last appearance at the Miss Texas Pageant, and the rumors and rumblings trickled back to me and my trainers. I was a clear contender this time, if not the projected winner.

After 365 days of working, training, singing, and focusing on creating the illusion of the perfect Miss Texas, it came down to that Saturday night in the Will Rogers Memorial Center. The top 10 contestants were announced, and I was one of them. We performed before a live Texas telecast, each of us smiling broadly and yearning for that ultimate validation. I was proud of my talent segment. I sang "Here's That Rainy Day," made popular by Frank Sinatra.

Then the final four were announced. At this point, your name is the last thing you want to hear because that means you didn't win. I heard it.

"The first runner-up is...Mae Beth Cormany."

In my mind, I was a loser, but by now, I knew how to flash that big smile and make it look genuine, so that's what I did on stage that night. It struck me that the song I had chosen couldn't have been more true.

Headed to Miss Texas, again I was devastated. Coming in as first runner-up was just too close for comfort. I felt I couldn't have tried any harder. The judges obviously thought Miss Denton was just plain better than Miss Fort Worth.

People told me not to take it to heart, but self-doubt ran through my head.: My voice wasn't strong enough. The song wasn't right. My evening gown was the wrong color. I failed the interview session. I wasn't smart enough, thin enough, tan enough. It tore right through my self-esteem. I had let people down. I was done.

So now what?

Some people weren't giving up on me, though, even if I already had. Pageant officials pitched the idea of running for Miss Texas again, this time as Miss Hurst-Euless-Bedford, representing the midcities between Dallas and Fort Worth. So here came the big question: *do I dare try again?*

Could I put myself out there a third time? The stakes were over the top now. After coming in as first runner-up, there was nowhere to go but up. The alternative was unthinkable. How could I possibly handle feeling like a failure again? After three years of tremendous dedication, work, and determination, I had discovered that pageants could be *fun*—as long as you're *not* in them.

The Miss Texas Pageant is the nation's largest preliminary to the Miss America Pageant. To my knowledge, it awards more scholarship money than any other state pageant. To me, however, the scholarship money didn't matter anymore.

Yes, it would help, because I was still enrolled at TCU—I would be a junior that year—but things had changed for me now. I had fallen into a dangerous groove and had no life other than chasing after that illusion of being perfect, or at least perfect enough to win Miss Texas. I entered the Miss Hurst-Euless-Bedford Contest with great trepidation and began what would be another 365 days of preparing for the final round—my last shot at the crown I somehow wanted so desperately now. My voice teacher, Helen Mashburn, put together a medley of two songs: Johnny Mathis's rendition of "Misty" and Judy Garland's famous "Come Rain or Come Shine."

As the months went by, the training came easier. After all, that's all I knew now. Striving for perfection had become my normal. A beautiful figure, a beautiful face, a beautiful voice—that's all my life boiled down to. That's all I was to the world—and to myself.

The local pageant night approached. The crowd seemed to know what was at stake. They cheered me on in every way, and I received flowers and cards of encouragement to boost my hopes. At last, the emcee called my name as the winner: Miss Hurst-Euless-Bedford 1972.

Now came the final ride on this emotional roller coaster. It was the summer of 1972. I arrived at the Miss Texas Pageant filled with fear and fervor like never before. I asked myself many times why I had put myself through this painful, exhilarating challenge once again. I had no answer then, and nor do I have one now.

Wednesday, Thursday, and Friday nights—the preliminaries—were gut- and heart-wrenching. Dozens of beautiful, accomplished young women practiced every day on stage, preparing for the live Saturday-night broadcast. We had to know exactly where and when to hit our marks. We learned the preshow performance for the audience and the short version for the televised show. We were all exhausted that week, our nerves frayed. I thought I should have been used to the pressure by now, but things were even more stressful than ever.

On the final night, my parents were in the audience. My sister, Elaine, had flown in from Europe to join them. The anxiety was indescribable as I prayed not to hear my name until the very last call. *What if it happens again?* came the whisper from inside me. *What if I lose?*

My name wasn't announced in the top four, however. This time, I heard the emcee call out, "And your new Miss Texas is...Mae Beth Cormany!"

Finally! The tears flowed—from me, my friends, my family, my supporters. I was Miss Texas 1972.

By now I had been trained and prodded for years to fit society's image, from what a good daughter should be to what it took to win one of the largest beauty contests in the country. I'd tried to please others by being what they said I should be, by embodying what they thought was devotion or talent or beauty. I was living my life based on other peoples' ideals. I had learned to excel at creating just the right illusion. So what did *I* think was true in life? Who was Mae Beth Cormany?

I realized that I didn't know.

Yet in spite of my fears, I had pushed and forced my way toward many accomplishments, and that trend would continue. Come rain or come shine, illusion was my intimate friend, my unavoidable companion. The illusion of perfect beauty had fooled me into setting an ideal for myself that would never hold up over the long run, but it also continued to dare and tempt me to go after what I thought I wanted.

By age 21, I had already begun to learn about the three *C*s of life: choice, chance, and change. I'd learned that only by *choosing* to take that *chance*, whatever it might be, would my life *change*. And change was what I wanted. I didn't want to end up hiding in my kitchen from the repo man or being the runner-up in life, but I had yet to learn other things: that beauty is in the eye of the beholder and that there's no such thing as perfection.

4

The Miss America Pageant and the Pleasures of a Ding Dong

Normal is an illusion. What is normal
for the spider is chaos for the fly.

—Morticia Addams

In the summer of 1972, the Vietnam War was in high gear. The draft was being enforced, and young men were being sent overseas to fight and die in the name of freedom. Like many Americans, I watched it all on the nightly news from the safety of my TCU dorm room. These were turbulent times here at home, too. Many people were protesting the politics behind the war—and other things: race, poverty, equality. These were the issues at the forefront. *Roe v. Wade* was before the US Supreme Court, though the landmark decision would not be handed down until the new year. The Women's Liberation Movement was in full force, and the Miss America Pageant was exactly what they were protesting. They had a point. Women parading across a stage in a swimsuit was not exactly the image of liberation.

Feminism was something I thought little about back then. By this time, I had learned how to walk, talk, dress, sit, eat, and smile—

all to become a winner. Often, I was told what to say and what to think. As pageant contestants, we were careful not to offend anyone. In reference to the women's movement, a favorite answer of mine was, "I believe in women's rights, but I still like a man opening the door for me."

Though the times were changing, that was still some people's definition of the perfect woman.

The summer before the Miss America Pageant, I had an amazing coach: a classy former model named June Graves. She was the manager of the Miss Hurst-Euless-Bedford Pageant. To completely immerse myself in preparation for the contest, I lived with her and her delightful husband, teenage son, and younger daughter. Spending my days with such a loving family was a wonderful experience.

But it wasn't easy. I slept on a daybed in the Graves's living room, with only the privacy of an accordion door protecting me from the main entrance hall. And there was a strict regimen to follow if I was to have any hope of doing well in the Miss America Pageant: I woke up early each day, ate a poached egg for breakfast, and headed to the gym for a workout. After that, it was an hour with the voice coach before heading home for lunch—a hefty slice of tomato over some cottage cheese.

Then I spent part of the afternoon in June's backyard—remember, this was before tanning salons or spray-on tan products. When June's son came home from high school football practice, I went jogging with him, though not by choice. (To this day, I'm not a runner!)

By the end of the day, I would be so hungry, my head would spin with the amazing smells wafting from June's kitchen. She was a great home-style Texas cook. Many nights, I sat at the Graves's table staring at the chicken-fried steak, mashed potatoes and gravy, and corn while I poked at my boiled piece of chicken on a small bed of lettuce. The pageant officials watched me closely, and I was dropping more weight.

That summer felt as though it lasted for *years*. I was thin, tan, and in amazing shape, but I went to bed hungry almost every night. I had a secret, though: I knew where June hid the Ding Dongs.

If you're not familiar with the pleasures of a Ding Dong, let me describe them to you. Ding Dongs are delicious, mouthwatering little chocolate cakes rolled over a creamy white icing center, and they're positively sinful, especially if you are trying to win a beauty pageant. So when I couldn't take the hunger anymore, after the lights were out at 10:00 p.m. and I figured everyone was asleep, I went on my secret mission into the kitchen.

The first obstacle was getting out of bed without making too much noise. Getting that accordion door to open quietly was a slow process. Once I cleared that obstacle, I tiptoed into the kitchen, laser-focused on that lower cabinet where I would find the high-light of my day. I would crouch down like a jewel thief in front of a locked safe and then reach my arm far back into the cabinet until my fingertips bumped up against one of those delicious Ding Dongs. Then I would pull out my prize.

Back at the accordion door, closing it slowly enough was torture. Finally, I would get back in bed, fling the sheets over my head, and, eureka! I made it! The final challenge was opening the wrapper qui-etly, an almost impossible task. Then it was pure pleasure. I would devour that Ding Dong and then, my tummy full, sleep like a baby.

Though it all sounds funny now, it was no laughing matter back then. Trying to become the perfect young woman was a grueling process, not for the fainthearted. By now, though, it had become second nature. I was used to shaping my reality—and my figure— around what everyone else said I should be.

In return for my resolute commitment, I earned scholarship money, which came in handy as I continued studying speech, and the Texas officials showered me with bonus gifts, an apartment for the year, a car, and an amazing wardrobe.

Three dress designers worked with me—the remarkable Les Wilk from Dallas and two gentlemen from El Paso: Guy and Rex. These incredible artists designed some twenty-five gowns just for my body. I must admit, it felt wonderful for people to give their opinions toward what would look better on my scrawny frame. It felt as though they cared about me. They certainly knew more than I did about what would look better and, most important, what would make me stand out from the other contestants. They knew how to present me as the whole package, the perfect woman.

On the other hand, it was very humbling to hear them critique my body as if I weren't even there, as if I were simply a mannequin. Sometimes, as on one afternoon when I stood in front of a mirror with just a slip on, surrounded by nine or ten so-called experts, it was downright disturbing.

"Well, she's got quite a long neck, so we can attach a collar to the dress," one said.

"What about these skinny arms?" asked another. "Let's cover up part of them, especially the elbows."

We humans can forget a lot of things in a lifetime, but all those negative remarks have stayed with me until this day. They checked every part of my body, right down to my teeth, yet I've always told myself that they were viewing me with both loving care and loyal determination, that they simply wanted their state and me to win Miss America. So what is the illusion? Did these designers view me as their trophy, or did they genuinely care about me? This struggle over authenticity and illusion would stick with me through my days as an anchor.

Judged from Stage to Anchor Desk

The summer I spent preparing for the Miss America Pageant was full of hope and hard work, but underneath all the tanned skin, fancy dresses, and learned poise was a growing personal crisis: How could I become the perfect woman? Whose opinion should I follow? I wanted to follow the advice of people I trusted, but everyone had a different opinion. June wanted me to wear my hair her way. The manager of the Miss Texas franchise had his own opinion. I was pulled back and forth. Whose concept of "perfect" should I ascribe to? Did anyone care what *I* thought?

Later in life, as I thought about the importance of image in the news industry, particularly among on-air personnel, it dawned on me that nearly everything these pageant specialists were creating was nothing more than an illusion to win the judges' and audience's approval, just as television consultants and station managers dream up a news anchor's image for ratings. Every news station would fly in its experts to tell us how to sit (*straight and tall says, "I'm trustworthy"*), what to do with our hands (*don't clasp them as if you're praying*), and the speed at which we talk (*the faster you speak, the more credible you sound*).

Like my pageant mentors who had never been Miss Anything, most of these consultants had never sat on the other side of an anchor desk. Many had never been reporters, but that didn't stop session after session of brutal critique and a never-ending catalogue of dos and don'ts.

I always have the same words of wisdom for young people who want to get into the television news business: *Be prepared. Your job is only as secure as ratings, research, and the news director.* Many times, the office you're sitting in has a revolving door. Even seasoned news anchors and reporters cringe when someone new takes over the station. New management never saw the years of dedication involved in writing documentaries, investigating news stories, performing harrowing live camera shots, or sitting up past midnight at the anchor desk as you wait for a ball game to be over so you can start the newscast, not to mention hostage situations, elections, or weekend parades. That was all part of the job—both as a news anchor and as Miss Texas—but so was looking good in the spotlight and seeming prepared under pressure. Like my pageant mentors, new management always had to put its own spin on the newsroom. Station owners and managers wielded godlike powers because they could. This included enforcing their idea of the perfect image of a female coanchor.

For many years, women were not supposed to wear short sleeves on camera because it wasn't professional to see our arms. Another no-no was to never, ever touch your coanchor. We were broadcasters, not humans. One consultant asked me not to move my eyebrows when I talked. How do you do that? No one, not even in the Miss America process, had ever complained about my misbehaving eyebrows.

But he handed me eye concealer to put over them anyway, and they didn't look brown anymore. They looked gray and gunky. *Is this really helping?* I wondered. *Will people see me as the perfect woman for the job?*

One station owner, after each newscast, would send little pink slips of paper with instructions written on them—things like, *I don't want to see your ear,* which meant he didn't want to see half my face turned away from the camera. The only solution, in his mind, was to cheat to the camera: turn one quarter of my face toward my fellow anchor. *Must* sit *just right to* be *just right* was the message I took away from this particular pink slip.

The debate about hair was just as heated in television news as it was on the pageant circuit. One news director who'd had a voice in hiring me, hairdo and all, brought me into his office to tell me my hair was too long. "It's too glamorous," he complained. "You can't deliver the news when you look too glamorous."

"Okay," I replied, eager to please. "I'll get it cut." And I headed to my hairdresser.

As is the nature of the business, it wasn't long before that director was fired. Shortly after the new director from Las Vegas took over, he brought me into his office. He punched up a newscast on a monitor and hit the pause button, pointing to my face. "What do you think is the most important thing about a news anchor?" he asked.

"Delivery?" I offered. "Believability? Credibility?"

He said no to each before giving me the "correct" answer. "It's your hair," he said profoundly. "Your hair is too short. You look like a dyke." As if that wasn't enough, he added, "And your eye makeup, it's too strong. You look like a hooker."

First, I was too glamorous; now, apparently, I had achieved the opposite extreme. Both a dyke and a hooker? How do you fix that image? Today, no news director would get by with that sort of name-calling, although the process behind it—the micromanagement of every physical aspect, whether you're a beauty queen or a news anchor—is still very much in practice.

How do you portray perfection when the very idea of perfection varies from person to person? Both men had different ideas about the illusion I was supposed to portray. And as the powers above me shifted, the standard of perfection changed, too, wavering before me like a mirage in the desert. In the news industry, as in the pageant circuit, my job depended on chasing someone else's idea of perfection. But perfection—what I'd been taught to seek my whole life, from being a good daughter to having what it took to win a beauty contest to fitting the image of an ideal female news anchor—was an impossible fantasy.

I would find out just how fragile that image was, almost a decade after the 1972 Miss America Pageant, when the illusion of perfection I had worked so hard to create at Channel 8 was shattered with just one uncharacteristic slip of the tongue.

From USO Troupe to New Christy Minstrels

September 1972 finally arrived. The Miss America Pageant was to take place in the Atlantic City Coliseum, along the famous Boardwalk facing the Atlantic Ocean. The runway, I was told, was the length of a football field. It was the last year the legendary Bert Parks would be emcee, the last year he would belt out, live on national television, "Here She Comes, Miss America." It was one of the most watched live TV shows of that time, garnering more viewers than both the Super Bowl and the World Series. But just a few years earlier, outside the coliseum—the epicenter of feminine perfection—women had protested the pageant by literally burning their bras.

The week was a tiresome blur, and by that Saturday night, I was enveloped in a fog. After making the top 10, having to sing on national television, and walking that football length runway in both a swimsuit and an evening gown, the time had come. The years of fantasies, hopes, setbacks, wins, and tears were about to come to an end. This was it!

Bert Parks called my name, but a few moments too soon. As third runner-up, I took my place to the side of the center circle. Miss Wisconsin, Terry Meeuwsen, was crowned Miss America 1973. I didn't win Miss America, but even so, my life was about to change forever: I was chosen to be part of the Miss America USO troupe.

That summer, we flew to Europe to entertain the American troops, visiting many army and air force bases in Germany and Holland. We performed in venues of all sorts, from two flatbed trucks pushed together in the middle of nowhere to the venerated Opera House in Munich.

One memory really stands out for me: visiting the Berlin Wall. We took a train at night that stopped at Checkpoint Charlie. We could hear the soldiers' footsteps coming down the aisles of the train as they checked each car, their guns held casually in front of them. We were all frightened, our hearts pounding in our ears, but their security check was uneventful. The train was allowed to go on.

In early 1973, when I got back from performing with Miss America USO, I got a surprising call from a world famous folk group called the New Christy Minstrels:

"Would you consider going on tour with us?" Ironically, they had lost their lead singer recently after she became the contestant who won Miss America: Terry Meeuwsen. Terry had sung professionally for years, and 1972 was the first year the pageant allowed professionals to enter the pageant. When she performed her signature song "He Touched Me" in Atlantic City, she brought the house down. And now they wanted me to replace her?

"Well, I'm not a belter," I told them. "Just sing something—loud!"

So I sang "The Star-Spangled Banner" over the phone as loudly as I could.

"You've got the job," they told me. "How soon can you be in Sacramento?"

I knew this was a great opportunity, and even if it wasn't exactly my dream come true, I don't think my old standby clichés would have let me off the hook.

The New Christy Minstrels were hitting the road in just a couple of weeks, so I had to learn a lot of music very quickly. The tour followed a horrendous schedule. We bounced all over the country, from coast to coast, on Braniff Airways. It was completely no-frills. We ate breakfast every morning on the plane. There were two other female singers and four male singers, including a travel manager. The two girls and I shared a room every night, alternating who got to sleep in the double and who got the rollaway bed. I didn't make much money—$187 a week, out of which came the cost of the hotel room and meals, but I got to see a lot of the country.

Life on tour wasn't easy. It was similar to the USO tour, though, and I was accustomed to working hard, chipping in to help set up and tear down for each performance, being part of a team. We performed six days a week and had just one day off. We each had one suitcase of clothes that had to accommodate snowy Toronto, Canada, one day and sultry Galveston, Texas, the next. At one point, we were in Toronto for two weeks for a ski exposition, and I was so happy to stay in one place for a while. That's when I knew I was just worn out.

For many years, I'd lived a life of being on the go. My voice was strained from singing, my face ached from smiling, and my body hurt from practicing and performing day and night. I was tired in every way. The illusion was wearing thin. I was ready to stop.

5

Tall + Dark + Handsome ≠ Love

If you want to live consciously, step out of the illusion.

—Beth Rengel

Once I'd decided I was finished with life as a singer, I made two phone calls: The first was to my parents, telling them I was coming back home to Texas. The second call was to my future husband.

During my year as Miss Texas, I had attended a ribbon-cutting ceremony in Dallas alongside some of the Dallas Cowboys NFL team and had become friends with defensive end Larry Cole. I mentioned getting a date with quarterback Craig Morton.

"He's not right for you, He's a womanizer!" Larry claimed. "But I have a really good friend in mind for you. His name is Mike Rengel. He played for the New Orleans Saints."

Larry introduced us, and Mike and I started seeing each other.

It was difficult because I was so busy—first as Miss Texas, then as a traveling performer, and he lived in New Orleans. I didn't get to know him very well, but he was tall, dark, and handsome, not to mention smart and kind. We dated long distance for a year. We made a terrific-looking couple. Well, that's what everyone said.

When I got off the plane in Wichita Falls, Texas, in the early winter of 1974, I was relieved that my touring days were over. I was exhausted, burned out, and tired of living out of a suitcase. I didn't know what would happen next in my life, and there at the airport, unexpectedly, was Mike. He had driven from New Orleans to surprise me—with an engagement ring.

I said yes, of course. It seemed like the right thing to do.

I had done it. I had convinced this man, and the good people of Texas, that I was the perfect woman. And surely, the rest—perfect husband, perfect marriage, perfect home, and perfect family—would follow, right?

Are Fairy Tales for Real?

In a perfect world, some romantics might think this was the beginning of the end of my story—a happy ending. After all, I thought being a wife and mother was all I'd ever wanted. That had been my goal growing up and in high school. In college, even though I studied as if to prepare for a career, like so many other young women of that time and place, I really expected to find myself a husband. All my life, I had collected recipes and photos, tearing pages out of magazines depicting what I wanted to cook or wanted my kitchen to look like. I no longer thought about being an architect as I had when I was a little girl, and, at this point, I had never even thought about a being on TV for a living. In truth, I never thought I had it in me. I just wanted to have three kids and drive a station wagon.

It was the perfect fairy tale: I was the good girl, and I had met a good man. We would live happily ever after, of course. That was what I wanted, wasn't it? I didn't want to shatter the illusion.

So rather than shatter the illusion, I went straight from touring with the Christy Minstrels to my next project: planning a wedding. Everyone was thrilled, except me.

In June 1974, days before the wedding, I went to my neighbors' house—a sweet retired couple. In truth, I hardly knew them, but I had to talk to someone. "I don't think I can do this," I confessed. "I just don't know what to do."

"Honey, it'll be okay," the older woman said. "But you need to talk to your mother about it." That was a horrifying thought. After all the wedding planning, how could I disappoint my mother? How could I ruin this epitome of the "perfect" wedding and marriage?

The night before the wedding, I finally built up the courage to open up to my mother. But when I retreated with her into the guest bathroom of our house, I was hardly able to open my mouth and let this horrid secret out. Finally, I managed to say, "I don't think I can do this. I don't love him."

After a long pause, my mother leaned over and patted my hand. "Oh, honey," she said, "you'll learn to love him."

I love my mother. She's always been my best friend, and I know she's always wanted the best for me, but her response left something to be desired—it's certainly not the kind of advice I would ever give to my own daughter. Perhaps you can learn to love a friend, a neighbor, a colleague, but, in my opinion, it would be hard to "learn to love" your spouse. Either that magic is there, or it's not—you can't create it.

At least, you shouldn't have to.

What was I to say? What could I do? My options seemed limited, so like a good girl, I sucked it up.

The wedding was to take place the next day at the First Baptist Church in Wichita Falls. The guests were all expecting the perfect wedding. Who was I to deny them?

At the appointed time, I found myself at the back of the church next to my dad. The music was playing. The groomsmen were all lined up at the far end of the aisle, staring at me. Mike, my fiancé, was beaming. The pastor of the church was waiting. All that was left was for me to walk down that long aisle.

I couldn't breathe, and I couldn't move. I stood at the back of the church in my white dress, grasping my father's arm. He was my last hope. So I dropped the bombshell. I looked up at him and said the same words I'd said to Mom the night before, "Dad, I don't think I can do this. I don't love him."

My dad looked down at me and said, "Now's a hell of a time to be telling me this! You see all those people who came to see you get married? Now get your ass down that aisle."

And like the good girl, I did.

What am I doing? I thought as "Here Comes the Bride" began to play, but I numbly walked forward, smiling my usual big smile. I knew how to do that. If only anyone had known what was going on inside me.

Then it was over. I was married. My only thought was, *Oh, God, what have I done?*

That night after the wedding, we drove to Dallas, where we would catch a flight the next day to Lake Tahoe for our honeymoon. I don't remember anything about that night. I've successfully blocked the entire memory. Things must have seemed right to Mike. After all, I was a performer, well trained to do the right thing, but, in reality, I was scared to death. I didn't know what I was doing, in the marriage or in bed.

I don't remember much about the honeymoon either, but I recall in great detail what it was like to come home afterward. Mike had bought a house in a suburb of New Orleans called Kenner. When he unlocked the front door, I headed to the most distant room in the house, as if I could escape my new life. My hands landed on the windowsill, and there I stood, just staring out like some kind of scared, trapped animal.

What have I done? I thought. *What have I done?*

Life Stopped

So began my life in New Orleans as a married woman. Mike, who had retired from the NFL because of an injury, was a very smart and successful civil engineer. He worked a lot and traveled a lot. And me? Well, I did exactly what I had always planned to do when I got married: I collected recipes.

In those early months of marriage, I watched my world come to a screeching halt. I was ending a season of my life that had been incredibly focused and goal-driven. For many years, competing in the pageant circuit, performing as a singer and dancer, and acting as an ambassador had required all my time and dedication. Even after the constant succession of pageants and the Miss America USO show, touring with the New Christy Minstrels had kept me going from goal to goal, one tour destination at a time. But now that I lived in New Orleans, my life was completely shifted around. The constant drive that had propelled me so far just suddenly ran out.

My life stopped.

Moving to a new city, being married, becoming a homemaker—it was all such an abrupt and drastic change. I was in a new place. I missed my friends. I missed my home state of Texas. I had been on a whirlwind tour of life, a merry-go-round of adventures, achievements, and experiences. Now, all of a sudden, I had lost my sense of identity. I had neither goals nor hope. I was Mrs. Rengel, and that was my entire identity.

So once again, I tried very hard to be who I thought I was supposed to be in that phase of my life. I stuffed my feelings into that emptiness left behind by my previous life—crammed them far down, trying to ignore them. To replace those feelings and regain some semblance of control over my life, I developed eating disorders—anorexia and bulimia—before everybody even knew they had names. I was lost and unhappy, and now I also felt like a failure at being a good wife, because I didn't want to be there. I felt empty.

I tried new recipes. I tried to make new friends. I even tried to get pregnant. I continued to work out because I was used to that. It was all I had left of the old me. But somehow, this white-picket-fence future wasn't all I'd imagined it to be. I would make cookies, binge eat, and then…well, you know. If I kept eating the way I felt, I couldn't stay skinny and maintain the illusion, even though I didn't know who I was maintaining it *for*.

I did some modeling in New Orleans, but I was never skinny enough to be a professional model. I just couldn't figure out how to reinvent myself or how to adjust. I was terrified because, no matter how much Mike wanted me to be happy and wanted us to be a happy couple, I simply couldn't see a happy ending.

My mother couldn't understand why I wasn't happy. After all, I had everything *she* had ever wanted. She sent me bewildered letters as if she could shame me into realizing that my marriage was perfect and my life was happy. "What more do you want?" her letters would say. "You have everything a young woman could want: a handsome husband, a beautiful home, a Mercedes, a country club membership…Now learn to play bridge."

People can grow to accommodate each other. I held on to that possibility for a while, thinking something might happen that would change things for Mike and me, for our marriage. But love? It wasn't happening.

A New Journey

What could I possibly find to do in this married life? I had run out of ideas. Luckily, someone else had an idea for me, something I never would have dreamed of.

I used to do commercials during high school and college for the owner of a Wichita Falls television station. This man tracked me down through my mother, found me in New Orleans, and asked whether I would be interested in auditioning for the weekend news anchor position at his other TV station in Amarillo, Texas.

I talked it over with my mother, who was not so keen on the idea. She did not want me to work outside of the home.

"If you take a job like that," she warned me, "it will damage your marriage."

I didn't take the station owner up on his offer, but the fact that he had even considered me for the job thrilled and electrified me. Though I didn't know it at that moment, his question had changed my life. It planted the seed. Suddenly, I could remember what it was like to have a goal and a purpose. I didn't want to spend weekends in hot, dry Amarillo, but his invitation got me thinking.

Me? A news anchor? Could I be a reporter? Could I possibly do that?

The station owner saw in me something I did not see in myself. He had confidence in me that I didn't know existed. And that confidence started the journey to where I am today.

It would take a long time before I could admit to myself that my journey in life would not include my first husband, and even longer before I could admit it to him and the rest of the world. I cared for Mike and have never stopped caring about him. His kindness was complete, and his attitude toward me never less than stellar, but I knew our "perfect" marriage would never be a reality.

Several years after we were married, sadness and guilt were the emotions most familiar to me. Mike and I didn't talk much about the marriage falling apart, though eventually he would realize it, too.

In the meantime, I tucked away the Wichita Falls station owner's offer in some corner of my brain, where it stewed and brewed inside me until I had to let it out. *A career as a news anchor,* I mused. *Why not?*

I had studied speech in college. I enjoyed public speaking. I'd loved writing since the seventh grade. I had experience being in front of the camera. So it all started to come together. It seemed as though I had a calling after all.

I began studying news broadcasts. I watched every anchor and reporter like a hawk, eager to learn what they did and how they did it. After all, imitating the experts and adopting a certain posture and poise was business as usual for me by now. I kept saying to myself, *I can do that! I can do that!*

Television journalism was still a male-dominated profession in the mid-1970s, but I became obsessed with watching the few women who had broken into the industry. My favorite was Jessica Savitch, an esteemed and award-winning female anchor for *The NBC Nightly News.* She was a commanding, beautiful blonde in her early thirties. She appeared to be very smart and had true presence. I watched her every move. I knew the way she sat, how she turned and tilted her head, her hand gestures, and the lilt in her voice.

Jessica made love to the camera. That's the only way I can describe it. She was *that* good. She captured your attention, and you hung on to every word she said, so, naturally, I practiced copying her.

I began creating the illusion of being a respected, knowledgeable female anchor like Jessica Savitch. In my mind, I became that person. If I was going to achieve this goal, I definitely couldn't be me, but I could pretend to be *her.*

6

Stupid Courage

No matter how you feel, you get up,
dress up, show up, and never give up!

—Beth Rengel

I had discovered in myself the drive to develop a career in news-casting, and it was the beginning of a new challenge and a new life. *Onward and upward*, was my thinking.

So I had a new project to tackle: getting my first job in TV news as a reporter. New Orleans had three TV stations. I found out the names of the news directors at all three stations and made appointments with each of them. I was armed with my videos of commercials from Texas and my public-speaking résumé from TCU. Would it be enough to launch my TV journalism career?

The first news director sat with me for ten minutes before ushering me out the back door. "Can't hire you without experience," he said matter-of-factly.

The second news director did the same.

At the final interview, as the chuckling news director showed me the door, I balled my fists and, without thinking, turned back to face him. "So how do I get experience?" I asked.

The man shrugged. "Go to a smaller market, like Baton Rouge."
He probably thought he was wasting his breath, but I clung to his
advice like a drowning sailor in a storm.

Divine Intervention

It was 1976, and Baton Rouge had two stations. I set up an interview at the ABC affiliate, WBRZ, for 10:00 a.m. on a Tuesday. I
would have to drive an hour and a half from New Orleans to Baton
Rouge on Lake Pontchartrain Causeway, the fastest way to travel
between the two cities—and still the world's longest bridge over
continuous water.

That morning, I made the unnerving drive through a torrential
rainstorm. My windshield wipers couldn't keep up with the rain,
and on either side of the causeway, I could see the dark, choppy
gray waters of the lake. With drivers unable to see the cars just
feet in front of them, traffic crawled, so I was running late. When I
finally found WBRZ, it was ten thirty. The rain was still hammering the pavement, and I had no umbrella. I wasn't sure what to do.
Should I wait for the rain to let up? Or should I just *run* in?

You've got to get in there, I thought. *You're late already.* My trusty
clichés were in full swing. If I didn't get in there right away, I'd
regret it, so I parked the car in the driving rain, opened the door,
and ran through the downpour into the building.

I was wearing a cobalt blue silk dress and more hairspray than
a 1960s singing group. Well, you probably know what silk does
when it gets wet. The wet marks spread, of course, and my hair
was a sticky mess. When I burst into the ice-cold, air-conditioned
lobby, drenched in a silk top...yes, they did! Folding my arms over
my chest and wiping the water from my face, I tried to summon
some composure.

"I have an appointment with John Spain, the news director," I
managed.

The receptionist just stared for a moment. "Oh. Yes, um…they're waiting for you," she replied.

I was embarrassed. This was not part of the plan. I did not look my best. How would I be able to sell myself as an on-air personality? But I straightened my spine into my best pageant posture, squared my shoulders, and marched right into the control room.

Trying to ignore the situation, I handed my videotape to the news director and the owner of WBRZ. They watched it, then looked at me—and started laughing.

"We don't hire anyone unless they have experience," John Spain explained.

My jaw dropped. That excuse again? But I had come here, to the smaller market of Baton Rouge, to *gain* experience. I felt anger rising in me. And suddenly something hit me—was it gut instinct or divine intervention? I don't know why, but suddenly I felt bold.

"Okay," I blurted out. "Then hire me for six months. I'll work for free. If you don't like me, then you can fire me."

It was one of my bravest, most calculated moments, and all the time I was thinking, *Where did that come from?* Perhaps it was that stupid, relentless courage we have when we're younger, before it fades away as a result of insecurity or rejection. Later, I would wonder if that little voice had always been there, buried so deep I didn't know I had it within me.

John Spain and his boss seemed to look at me through fresh eyes, maybe even with a hint of respect for the drowned rat who said she was a former Miss Texas. Then they looked at each other and whispered back and forth a little.

"Okay," John said. "You're on."

And with that, I became a television news reporter…who had no idea what she was doing. I had positioned myself as a career woman. Now could I pull off this masquerade? I didn't know, but I would soon find out.

Yet again I had to ask, *Oh, Lord, what have I done?*

My Television Career Begins

From that day forward, I started paying my dues at WBRZ. Every day I was up at 6:00 a.m., out the door before seven and, after driving more than an hour from New Orleans to Baton Rouge, across Lake Pontchartrain, at the office by eight.

My very first day, I walked in through the back door during the morning staff meeting. Everyone was turned away from me, so I had a view of the broad back of Bob Courtney, the capital correspondent, as he stood up and asked the news director, "Where's this so-called ex–beauty queen you just hired?"

The room full of men rumbled with laughter.

John Spain, however, had seen me come through the door. "Well, she just walked in," he said with a chuckle, pointing to where I stood behind all of them.

"Meet our new reporter: Beth Rengel, former Miss Texas."

What an introduction. Everyone turned around slowly. There I was, the new kid on the block, already saddled with a giant label on my forehead. It was going to be hard enough being the only woman in the newsroom, but now I would really have to live up to the hype.

Did the other reporters and newsroom staff give me the cold shoulder? You bet they did. I was the ex–beauty queen. In a way, I can't blame them for objecting to me. I had been hired despite having no experience. Right away, I realized that I had to work twice as hard in order to prove myself.

A new segment was created for me: "On the Road with Beth Rengel." This meant I had to get into a van with a cameraman by 8:30 a.m. and drive off to somewhere else in Louisiana. I was teamed up with the station's chief photographer, Vietnam veteran Mike Haley. He wasn't at all happy that I had been hired, and I knew what he was thinking: *Stupid beauty queen, wannabe reporter…*

Regardless, I was so proud of my first story. It was about an old, vacant, gorgeous Louisiana mansion that was going to be restored.

Mike Haley taught me how to appear confident in front of the camera and talk from memory. In the news world, this is called a *stand-up*. In the pageant world, it was par for the course, so I had that part down. But then I had to fill in the holes by writing the actual story.

Haley was not impressed. He was downright irritated. "I didn't shoot that!" he grumbled. "I can't put pictures to this." He squared off toward me. "What did you see me take pictures of?"

"Well...I...I...," I stammered. "The gazebo?"

"Then start with the gazebo," he replied gruffly.

He isn't trying to be mean, I kept telling myself, but it sure felt as though he was. Under Haley's instruction, I learned how to write to match the video footage. I figured out what would visually carry the story. In fact, he taught me everything I know about reporting. "Bullet Beth" became my nickname, because Haley taught me how to ask the hard, direct questions in interviews on tough stories.

After a time, Haley became more patient because he knew I was trying so hard, and his friendship is one I value even today. His on-the-job training paid off, both in Baton Rouge and for the rest of my career. I worked hard, I paid my dues, and I learned quickly. Six weeks after my first dubious day as a reporter, WBRZ hired me.

I had gambled on myself, on my disguise as an able TV journalist, and I had won. I still don't know where that sudden courage came from. Who offers to work for free? But if I hadn't made that offer, I never would've gotten my foot in the door. My facade of courage had been my first step toward being taken seriously. I had to prove that I could be just like the guys in the newsroom.

It was there at WBRZ that I started reinventing myself. I was no longer Miss Texas or Mrs. Rengel, identified only by an assumed name. I was Beth Rengel, reporter, and I had to prove myself as a newsperson. The staff had their own opinions of me based on their illusions about pageant contestants and what a former Miss Texas was. I had to single-handedly tear down that identity, rebuild a new one, and change their opinion.

I worked twice as hard, and slowly but surely, I became more than just a pretty face. I became a respected reporter. Eventually, Mike and I moved to Baton Rouge, so I no longer suffered through that hour-and-a-half-long commute in each direction, but I still put in long days and clocked countless driving miles. As a reporter in Baton Rouge, I did many stories in neighboring New Orleans and all around the different parishes of Louisiana. One late afternoon, I traveled to New Orleans to do a story you could only find in the Big Easy, about a man who was a Catholic priest by day and a saxophone player in the city's blues clubs by night. I met my photographer at one of the fanciest hotels on Bourbon Street. We set up in the bar to see this priest perform with his band.

It was close to 9:00 p.m. when we wrapped up, and I was finally heading back home to Baton Rouge. About halfway down the causeway across Lake Pontchartrain, I looked in my rearview mirror and saw a long black limousine cross the center line into the oncoming lane. It sped up, passed my car, and then swerved back into the lane in front of me. Then another limousine sped up behind me and got right up snug, just inches from my back bumper.

What was going on? Needless to say, I was frightened. This was before cell phones and automatic car door locks. I was driving my little red 1972 Mercedes 280 SL, a two-seater, and I was sandwiched between these two big cars. I was boxed in.

When the limo in front of me started slowing down, I had to do the same. I had no choice. My heart was pounding. Was someone going to drag me out of my car and push me over the side of the bridge into this dark, deep lake?

At last, all three vehicles came to a stop. I snuck a peek over my shoulder and saw a silver-haired man in a black suit jump out of the backseat of the limo behind me. He ran toward me and stopped just outside the passenger side of my car. Then he opened the door and got in, looking at me and…smiling?

It was Governor Edwin Edwards.

He reached into his left inside suit pocket, pulled out a piece of paper, and started unfolding it. I didn't know what to think. Was I in some sort of trouble?

Then the governor of Louisiana began to read aloud a poem he had written—*for me*.

I didn't hear a word he read. I was in complete shock. My heart was still hammering from the way the limos had forced me to pull over. Not only that, but his overpowering cologne distracted me, filling my head—and my car.

I kept looking at his slicked-back gray hair, his stiff white shirt, his creased black suit. I couldn't get past the dizzying scent of his cologne, much less the question of what in the world he was doing in my car. I had *not* invited him to get in. If he'd taken the liberty of scaring me half to death by pulling me over and then hopping in my car to read a poem, what *else* would he feel was within his rights and his power? Most people don't do things like that—unless they feel as though they can.

My hands, white-knuckled, never left the steering wheel. When the governor finished reading his poem, he refolded it, put it back in his pocket, and then, in his Cajun accent, said, "Now, Miss Beth, you come see me at the mansion tomorrow morning, d'ya hear?"

I nodded my head yes.

With that, the governor got out of my car and walked back to his limousine. The limo in front of me started forward, and I followed. We caravanned back toward Baton Rouge. At the end of the causeway, we went our separate ways.

I called the next day to make sure I was supposed to go to the governor's mansion. They said he was expecting me. I cleared it with my news director. We were hoping for a scoop, some big exclusive story, but when I got there, it was nothing like that. The governor simply wanted me to have lunch with him there at the mansion. I was too uncomfortable to stay, so I excused myself politely and left.

Governor Edwards, who served four terms as governor and, before that, four terms as a US congressman, has the reputation of being one of the most corrupt governors in American history. Aside from his alleged connections to the Mafia, he was a notorious womanizer. Ultimately, he was convicted and sent to prison on several felony charges stemming from a casino license scheme. Released in 2011 after an eight-year prison term, he ran for US Congress once more in 2014 and, in his late eighties, actually beat the Democratic contenders in the primary, though he lost to the Republican candidate in the runoff election. This was a powerful man who was used to getting what he wanted. And we all know how easy it is to get caught up in someone else's illusion of power.

As I drove back to the TV station that day in 1977, I couldn't help but wonder at the governor's audacity. As a woman, I was slightly flattered by his singling me out, but above all, I was saddened by his abuse of power. Here was a career politician, a man with great influence, and he was using it for his personal whims. I have no doubt that he was quite impressed with himself and the persona of power and influence he'd gathered about him. He'd gotten carried away with his own legend, but when you scrape away all the layers and get down to the basics, beneath the illusion of power, there's still just a man under it all.

We all want to trust the leaders we vote into public office, but we must ask ourselves if we can see through the illusion they create because often, much of what we see is nothing more than a mirage.

Bona Fide

As a rookie reporter, I covered many compelling stories about Louisiana's culture and history, stories that—like my encounter with Governor Edwards—revealed the particularly intriguing nature of that part of the country. I also had the chance to substitute as an anchor from time to time, which at last provided the irreplaceable experience I needed to advance my career. What had started as posturing and bluffing my way into the newsroom turned into quite the opposite: I was becoming the real thing.

Eventually, I overcame the "beauty queen" label at WBRZ and felt like a bona fide reporter. I had to fight for every legitimate hard news story. I had to plead my case and demonstrate why I should be the one to cover First Lady Rosalynn Carter's trip to New Orleans. I had to beg to cover one of the worst oil spills in the Gulf of Mexico and the documentary called *Little Alcatraz of the South*, about Angola State Penitentiary. All that taught me the perseverance to fight for who I had become. I learned to peel back the illusions and listen for my own voice.

Through my developing career, I had found a new identity, one that I'd chosen for myself and achieved on my own. I'd found a purpose and a passion outside of my marriage. The eating disorders subsided, but my body was dealing with another health issue now.

To fit in with the guys in the newsroom, I'd tried to learn how to smoke cigarettes. I soon learned that I wasn't a smoker. Smoking made me sick, and I couldn't sleep at night. I would take over-the-counter sleeping pills, but then I couldn't wake up in the morning. So I started to take over-the-counter diet pills to get moving. Why didn't I just quit smoking? It would have been a lot easier than living in that vicious cycle, but part of me just thought it was part of the image of a career journalist.

The stress of keeping up the facade of being a tough reporter and of living a lie in my marriage—had gotten to me. By the time I went to see a doctor, the pain was intense. When the doctor diagnosed me with a soon-to-be perforated duodenal ulcer, he called me at work and said, "Whatever you're doing, you need to stop right now. You're on the verge of having a bleeding ulcer."

I wasn't ready to make a real change just yet, though, until I got that advice from someone I'd known all my life.

That year, my sister came from Europe to visit me in Louisiana. "What happened to you?" she asked with a flabbergasted look on her face.

I was puzzled. "What do you mean?"

"Well, what happened?"

I don't know what tipped her off, but Elaine saw right through me. What I had so successfully hidden for four years of marriage didn't get past her. Finally, someone had noticed that something was *very* wrong.

I broke down and sobbed. When I could finally speak, I choked out, "I'm not happy in this marriage!"

Her words were short and direct: "Then get a divorce."

No one had ever been divorced in our family. I took my marriage vows very seriously. Get a divorce? The thought had never entered my mind, but somehow, my sister gave me permission to consider it.

I decided to leave Baton Rouge and get a job somewhere else. I saved up my vacation time and some money. I worked with headhunters and talked to talent scouts. I interviewed with news stations in Denver and Nashville. I felt sad and guilty about planning this secret departure from Mike. It was emotionally devastating because I still cared about him as a friend, but my marriage was killing me—or rather, by staying in the marriage, *I* was killing me.

The station owner in Wichita Falls had planted a dream in my heart. News director John Spain had given me a chance to chase after it. And photographer Mike Haley had taught me everything I needed to know about reporting. Together, these events became a God-sent opportunity, and now I knew I had the strength to grab hold of it and ride this journey to the end.

I was sad about what was coming: the inevitable end of my marriage. I was grateful to the folks at WBRZ who had helped me kick-start my career. Most of all, though, I was thankful because I knew in my heart that my life was changing. I had found a career that called to me, and I was going to find my own voice.

7

The Big Apple

Many of life's failures are people who did not realize how
close they were to success when they gave up.

—Thomas A. Edison

The illusion of the perfect career was calling me with its siren song:
the ballad of perfect success. My ambition and drive as a broadcast
journalist picked up right where the former pageant contestant had
left off. I was chasing fulfillment down the familiar road of success,
and before I could decide where the road would lead, there was one
stop I had to make: New York City.

"We've Got a Live One Here!"

I set up two interviews, one with the executive producer of NBC's
America Alive, a live program at the RCA Building (now the GE
Building), and the other with *ABC News*. I also scheduled a third
meeting: a casual, friendly lunch with an acquaintance from the
pageant world.

As often as I could, I watched *America Alive*, which aired at
11:00 a.m. with hosts Jack Linkletter (Art Linkletter's son) and his
cohost, Pat Mitchell. I was addicted to the show because I knew I

could do Pat's job. I just knew it. I simply had to meet the executive producers of the show, Ken Greenglass and Woody Fraser. The detective skills required for my new career came in handy. By watching the credits roll at the end of the live program, I found out their secretary's name: Chickie.

So I gathered up my courage and called Chickie. "I'm Beth Rengel from Baton Rouge, an old friend of Woody's and Ken's," I fibbed. "I'm going to be in town, and I'd love to see the show." Yes, in my mind we were longtime friends because I'd been watching their show for years.

"Oh, sure!" Chickie replied. "Come see the show. Woody is in Los Angeles, but you can see Ken after the show."

At 10:00 a.m. on a Tuesday in June 1978, I was ready to take the next step toward success. Looking sharp with my briefcase in hand, I entered the RCA building, weaving my way through the disorderly line of people waiting to see the show. A page met me—and helpfully showed me to the back of the line.

This is going nowhere fast, I thought.

But once again, a sudden boldness came over me. Out of nowhere came that alternate personality who had shown up in Baton Rouge a few years earlier. I straightened my posture, put on my pageant smile, and turned to the page.

"I'm sorry," I told him, "but I'm Beth Rengel from WBRZ in Baton Rouge, and I have to be up there before the show starts—and that's not going to happen if I'm at the end of this line."

"Oh," said the young man, and a sheepish look came over his face. "You're Beth Rengel from Baton Rouge? Here, follow me."

We hopped in an elevator and went up to the eleventh floor. He took me to the green room where the show's guests were waiting to go on set. It was Cher's mother and the redheaded star Katherine Helmond from the 1970s prime-time series *Soap*, both of them with their younger boyfriends. That's when I found out the topic of the show: the trend of older women being attracted to and dating younger men. Now we call them cougars, and it's not such a risqué topic anymore, but back then, it was practically taboo.

The audience members were filling up the studio. I wanted to be front and center to get Ken Greenglass's attention, so I headed into the seating area, too. I caught the cameraman's eye. "Can I sit here?" I asked him.

"Sure," he replied.

So there I sat in the middle of the front row, facing the stage. Soon after I settled in, they got the live show going, with the music and everything else. Jack Linkletter gave his customary greeting and introduced the day's hot topic. They went through the entire first segment, and then Jack called for a break, announcing that next he'd be asking the audience what we thought about all older women dating younger men.

As soon as the show returned from break, Jack opened it up for questions.

"Does anyone have anything to say?" he asked.

And lo and behold, there went my arm, popping right up in the air!

"We've got a live one here!" Jack said with a smile. "Would you stand up and introduce yourself?"

Pasting a sure and confident smile on my face, I said, "I'm Beth Rengel from Baton Rouge." I'd never dated a younger man, but I pretended to know what I was talking about. "I'd like to make an observation. You can't just generalize and say that all younger men are attracted to older women and that older women are attracted to younger men. Look at all the men in this audience. Are they attracted to older women?"

Jack picked up on this point, and though I remember almost nothing else that I said, I'd accomplished my mission: In the control room, Ken Greenglass asked, "Who is that?"

Whether my conversations with Chickie, the secretary, or the young page ever came to light, I don't know, but when Ken's assistants came to find me afterward, I acted as though I had expected it. I ended up meeting with Ken for more than an hour, telling him about my experience and my goals, and he seemed convinced—though whether it was my résumé, my determination, or something else that did it, I'll never know. Though he didn't offer me Pat's job, he offered me a writing position on the show.

It was a great opportunity, and I considered it carefully…before turning it down. I had a one-track mind. I could envision only one path to my success: I wanted to be on the air.

Me on a Soap Opera?

A few years back, I had joined the judging panels for several preliminary state pageants and worked with one of the Miss America judges: the debonair Robert Dale Martin, a casting director for CBS's soap operas. He had told me, "Whenever you're in New York, call me. We'll have lunch." So I did.

We met at the Waldorf Hotel restaurant. Robert got right to the point. "Have you ever thought about being on a soap opera?" he asked.

I didn't want to be rude, so I just shook my head and said, "I'm a journalist."

After lunch, he gave me a brief tour of the CBS studios. We went to one of the soap opera sets, where he handed me a script. "Here, you read the part of Julie," he said. "I'll read the part of your mother."

I waved the script away, protesting, "Robert, I didn't even take acting classes in high school."

"Go ahead, let's practice," he insisted.

So we did. After a few times going over the scene together, he picked up the phone and mumbled, "Please come in for a minute."

A moment later, onto the set walked a large lady draped in a flowered dress. With hefty shoulders, thick forearms, and a square jaw, she looked like a woman who would portray a German milk lady from the 1920s—the furthest thing from a soap opera persona I could imagine. But as she leaned on the doorway, Robert seemed to take her cue. He gave me a nod and said, "Okay, let's go."

We read our parts. I have to admit I was scared, but it was also thrilling. The idea of taking on another person's identity, of trying to fill that person's shoes...

For a moment, I thought maybe this—being an actor, living in New York—was another route to the success I craved.

When we finished the reading, Robert looked back at the German milk lady, who nodded.

Robert looked back at me and said, "You have the part."

A part in a CBS soap opera! The excitement that ran hot-blooded through my veins just a moment ago suddenly froze into fear. A million thoughts raced through my head: *New York?*

Me, live in the Big Apple? Where would I live? It's so far away!

What about my job in Baton Rouge? What about getting the divorce?

Once again, I was flattered by the offer, but all the what-ifs overwhelmed me. I politely turned down the part.

In hindsight, I'll always wonder why the three clichés didn't kick in that time. Was I afraid of failing at something I knew nothing about? No, I had managed to bypass that fear once already in my career when I barged into WBRZ. Well then, was I afraid of success? I'll never know for sure. Either way, once again I was determined to continue on the path I had chosen.

Tulsa Bound

My last interview in New York was with Bill Fife, vice president of *ABC News*. I bluffed my way into that interview as well. Bill was a tall, dark-haired, soft-spoken man who actually looked at the tape of me reporting local news at WBRZ in Baton Rouge, one of the smallest markets in the country.

"You're good," said Bill after watching my tape, "but you're not ready for New York. This place will eat you alive."

I was disappointed, but I respected his opinion and told him I would be glad of any advice he could give.

"Go get a couple of years of experience in a medium-sized market, then come see me," he replied.

I was still thinking big. "You mean like Dallas or Chicago?"

"No," he said gently. "I was thinking Tulsa, Oklahoma."

My heart sank. "Tulsa?"

"Our affiliate KTUL is perfect," he continued. "I'll put you in contact with the station manager. Tulsa will be great for you."

As I left the ABC offices and stepped back out onto the Manhattan sidewalk, joining the crush of midtown pedestrians, one word flashed over and over in my head: *Tulsa? Tulsa?*

Tulsa…that's Oklahoma. But I'm from Texas. Between these two neighboring states, there exists a huge rivalry. College football fans from the University of Oklahoma proclaim that Texas is nothing more than "southern Oklahoma," and University of Texas fans, of course, call Oklahoma "north Texas."

I went back home to Baton Rouge deflated, broke, and out of vacation time. I felt defeated, but I had to move on. If not to New York, then maybe to Tulsa.

When I called Tom Goodgame, the KTUL station manager, I could almost hear him lean back in his chair, chewing on his cigar. "Well," he said, "we're just sick at losing Barbara, our anchor. We've viewed *at least* a hundred tapes. No one can take her place. But if you think you're good enough, go ahead and send me a tape."

That mysterious boldness, that divine intervention, kicked in again. I confidently told him, "I'm going to send you a tape today, and you're going to like it."

He got it, and guess what? He liked it.

I flew into Tulsa two weeks later and immediately fell in love not only with the city, but also with the Channel 8 crew. It was an amazing team—a real powerhouse of talent, with the tagline "8's the Place." No one else could compete with this local ABC affiliate, and I was glad to become a part of it. Maybe this was the next step along my path to success.

Suddenly, I was a newscaster.

It was the first time in my life I had made a decision entirely for myself, by myself, and, to this day, it is one of the hardest I've ever had to make. Mike knew I was unhappy and starving for my own personal identity once more. The guilt of the breakup was almost unbearable because making the decision to leave was totally against who I had grown up to be. There were many tears and painful moments, but I rationalized this separation by telling myself that Mike deserved a better wife. We were divorced in 1978.

I had started all over by leaving Baton Rouge, and now Tulsa became my new home. On the KTUL team—the "Dream Team"— were the legendary, handsome Bob Hower; beloved weatherman Don Woods; and charismatic, brilliant sportscaster Chris Lincoln. I knew I was the token female, but it was worth it. I was part of a respected and trusted news team, directed by the amazingly talented Carl Bartholomew.

Carl was an out-of-the-box thinker who created unprecedented commercials promoting KTUL, including spots with the team dressing up in character as cowboys, gangsters, Revolutionary War soldiers, go-kart drivers, Western stage coach travelers, and 1940s Hollywood stars. His idea was to have me do a weekly series called *Lifestyles.*

"Beth, we need to get you out in the field, dirty, sweaty," he explained, "and get you out of your prim and proper image."

So I showed the Tulsa audience what it was like to drive an eighteen-wheeler, be a conductor on a traveling train, and be a pet groomer, to name a few. The most frightening segment was when I scaled down the tallest building in Tulsa to show what it's like to be a window washer. My photographer talks about it to this day. The shoot that day involved me hanging fifty stories above downtown Tulsa, trying to maintain my composure as I swayed back and forth in the wind.

I spent some two and a half years with KTUL, enjoying getting windblown by day and trying to portray the illusion of perfection by night. My days started at noon and ended at 11:00 p.m. Our ratings were through the roof. But that illusionary bubble popped in an instant—the instant I cursed on the air.

8

Fired to Hired

A woman is like a tea bag. You never know how strong she
is until she gets in hot water.

—Eleanor Roosevelt

What should be done with Beth Rengel?

It seemed this was the question on everyone's lips, from Tulsa
to Timbuktu, after my fateful broadcast mishap in February 1980.

The local newspapers ran with the saga, slapping on headlines
like "TV Anchor Suspended for Cursing on Air." My unfortunate
slip of the tongue even made some national newspapers. This was
before the Internet, of course, so the wire copy was our only source
of immediate news. And this so-called news made the Associated
Press wire copy in every newsroom in every city with a TV station,
as far as Alaska.

What should be done with Beth Rengel? It was the latest buzz, and
it lasted for days. The local radio talk show hosts, in particular, ate it
up. My career was the fresh meat they needed to keep callers coming, the newest controversy to liven up their shows. Meanwhile, I
was suspended and had nothing else to do with my time but worry.
My job was in mortal jeopardy. I couldn't sleep. I couldn't eat. I
found myself curled up in the fetal position on the kitchen floor by

the telephone, waiting for the call, crying and unable to get up or move. I felt paralyzed.

What have I done?

The calls had started coming in right away. Some people said that I'd called it right about the newscast being such a fiasco, that I should not have cursed, but my mike should not have been open, either. Most callers, though, were downright angry at what they'd heard.

I asked the station's operator to get the names and addresses of anyone who was upset. I was kicking myself. I should have followed my instincts and made an apology right then and there, on the air, but instead, with Bob Hower there to guide me, I had fallen back on my old habit: I did what I was told to do. So now I intended to write an apology to each and every person who'd called to complain. I felt the need to make it up to them somehow. What else could I do?

I couldn't get my mind off what I'd done. My face had been on thousands and thousands of televisions in Tulsa and the surrounding communities, so now I couldn't even go to the grocery store without people (usually women) pointing, covering their mouths, and whispering. I tried going to a restaurant one time, but when I walked in, it seemed as though everyone stopped talking and stared at me. My most embarrassing moment had been very, very public, and I hid myself from the infamy.

This was more than a simple mistake, more than just a gaffe. People were deeply offended. It was especially traumatic for me because I was not brought up to use such language, particularly in public. That's not who I was or who I am today. And now my career was in danger because of it. That perfect success I'd been hoping for and working toward was beginning to look very much out of reach.

I had a decision to make: Was this the end of my career? Or would I get back up and go forward? I had worked so hard to establish a credible reputation. In the late 1970s and early 1980s, women newscasters had to work twice as hard and fight for any legitimate story. In an industry dominated by men, we didn't have much of a voice in the newsroom. Every woman who made it to the anchor chair added another win in the fight for equal opportunity. Somehow, it seemed as though giving up would be tantamount to taking a step backward in that struggle.

The station owner, Mr. Leake, had to make a similar decision: What should be done with Beth Rengel? Should she be fired or let back on the air?

I was surprised and relieved to learn that I had some support in the community. I saw a billboard that said "8's Not the Place without Beth Rengel." There was even a bomb threat accompanied by a warning to the station to reinstate me. But all this did little to help my mood. I didn't know how long I would be suspended, or if I even had a job anymore. I called Mr. Leake repeatedly, but he wouldn't return my calls.

Some employees at the station knew I was trying to reach Mr. Leake, and one of the secretaries called to let me know he was in the building.

"I need to talk to him," I pleaded, so she put me through. When he picked up, I said, "Mr. Leake, I am so sorry. I just have to apologize. This is so...not me! Please, I need to know...do I still have a job?"

"I don't know," he replied. "We're still thinking about it."

But I couldn't bear the waiting any longer. "I'm sorry, sir, but that's not fair," I persisted. "I can't keep going with this big dark cloud over me. Think about it, how would you feel?"

"Since you're taking that attitude about it," he came back, "come and get your things and your severance pay."

I'd just been fired.

I don't even remember if I went back to get my personal things from my desk at KTUL. I was devastated. Things just went blank.

George, the news director, resigned after sticking up for me. The weekend anchor took my place, and the news flurry over my mishap slowed down. Newer, more sensational stories edged out the story of the infamous anchor who cursed on live TV, and I could shop for groceries and go out to eat in restaurants again. But the intense embarrassment that I felt didn't fade. In fact, I experienced something I've never truly felt before—shame.

I cried a lot, thinking my career was over. I spent many sleepless nights with embarrassment as my only companion. Though it was unintentional, I felt that I had let many people down. What's worse, I never got a chance to explain or apologize to the people of Tulsa. Though I had handwritten an apology to every viewer who called in to complain, I felt no absolution.

I had always been grateful for the trust the viewers put in me. I never took the job lightly. Part of the job, from my point of view, was to project that illusion of a strong anchorwoman, portraying confidence and reporting the unbiased news of the day. Part of this, I thought, was wearing the perfect clothes, shoes, and hair. Why not? I had invested years in trying to pursue that perfect image. Now the façade of perfection had cracked, and my career, my reputation, and my chances at success were all tainted.

Maybe TV news wasn't for me. After almost five years of being in the business, I thought maybe I should call it quits, try a new career, search for anonymity. But through all the pain, humiliation, and self-doubt, I kept going back to those three choices: give up, give in, or get back up.

For someone whose vocabulary does not include the word *quit*, getting back up was the only option.

The illusion was shattered—Beth Rengel wasn't perfect. I had failed in my career, and on the other side of life, I felt like a failure in relationships, too. I was a divorced woman now. Working five nights a week with Channel 8 had left only Saturday nights to live like other people did. When you're in that kind of business, it's hard to have a personal life. I had totally given up on a second chance at finding love.

I ended up dating one man most of the time I lived in Tulsa. Milton Berry was twelve years older and seemed to enjoy the fact that I was the new girl in town and had a high-profile job. He swept me off my feet, but the relationship was rocky from the get-go. Loving someone and falling in love, in my mind, are two different feelings. I was crazy in love, and when it's not reciprocated, that's the most uncontrollable, insecure, and lonely feeling in the world. I felt I never could quite get his approval in anything I did, even anchoring the news.

It occurred to me that I might remarry someday and be introduced to a whole new world: motherhood. That was the last thing on Milton's mind. He had married twice before and had five children already. He was successful in Tulsa's oil boom days of the late 1970s and early 1980s, and he was loving his freedom.

Still, though I was working in Tulsa to achieve my career goals and create that illusion of perfect success, I began to feel once again the pull of the white picket fence. At the almost doomed age of thirty, I began to wonder, What was life like on the other side of that fence?

Next Stop, Atlanta

At the time of the Channel 8 firing, Milton and I had broken up. I wanted a commitment, and he didn't. Shortly afterward, I took a job as news anchor for KGCT-41 Live, a first-of-its-kind local TV station broadcast on the Tulsa Cable News Network from the downtown district. Several high-profile radio and on-air personalities jumped on board, too. We hit the air in September 1980. Owner Ray Bindorf was ahead of his time, offering live, local news and entertainment all day long. The broadcast only lasted several months before shutting down because of a lack of funds to support this new TV idea, so, for me, it was back to the drawing board.

After the mishap at KTUL, I felt like everyone thought of me as the news anchor who had cursed during a live broadcast. But I wasn't going to let my dream of being an anchor die with my time at Channel 8 and my most embarrassing professional moment. I had to heal and restore my sense of purpose, but probably not in Tulsa. My recovery and rebirth would have to happen somewhere else.

I got in contact with a headhunter, sent out tapes with samples of my on-air work, and quickly landed a job in Atlanta as the anchor for the 5:30 p.m. weekday newscast on the NBC affiliate, WXIA. With this move, I went from the country's fiftieth-largest market to the eleventh-largest.

In Atlanta, as elsewhere, it was a male-dominated business, from management to sales to engineers to anchors. I was the only female anchor on the any of the weekday newscasts: 5:30 p.m., 6:00 p.m., and 11:00 p.m. I was driven and determined to succeed, and within six months, I was promoted to primetime, the 6:00 p.m. newscast, replacing Dave Michaels to sit next to anchor John Pruitt.

My coanchors at 11-Alive did very little to contribute. They were viewed as on-air personalities. As I recall, John would read the newspaper until it was time for the broadcast, and Dave (who had moved to another time slot) would do crossword puzzles to pass the time. Often, I would offer to write articles, but the producer would shake his head no while never even looking up. I found myself feeling guilty for not helping out and would try to look busy when we were off the air—crazy, isn't it? But that's the way it was.

I did manage to develop a weekly series called *Wednesday's Child* that was popular in several markets. It spotlighted children who were available for adoption. Part of the series required my photographer and me to take the children to fun places like the zoo, the park, or the lake to ease the children's fears of being on camera. It was a good cause, and it got me out of the stuffy newsroom and into the beautiful and vibrant city of Atlanta.

Atlanta is an electric city that boasts culture, historic neighborhoods, great food, and beautiful seasons. It's also a huge sports city that particularly loves its famed NFL franchise, the Falcons. Every night at 11-Alive, I sat next to Harmon Wages, a former Falcons player and the sportscaster during our 5:30 p.m. newscast. We made many appearances together as part of the news team, but he was dating the CBS affiliate WAGA's weekend anchor, Deborah Norville. I was dating a good friend, former Minnesota Vikings and New York Giants quarterback Fran Tarkenton. One of the nicest and funniest gentlemen in Atlanta, Fran was aware of why I'd left Tulsa with so much unfinished business. In fact, he was the only one in Atlanta in whom I confided while contemplating a return to Tulsa. I remember our conversation, sitting at one of the most beautiful bars in Atlanta.

"Don't do it," he said. "Don't go back to Tulsa."

He said "Tulsa," but I knew he meant Milton. "Just remember," Fran told me, "a leopard never changes its spots."

The Hatchet Man

I had been working in Atlanta for more than a year and had bought a condominium in a posh area called Buckhead when the general manager who hired me got promoted. His temporary replacement came from the company's Denver affiliate, accompanied by rumbles of doom and gloom throughout the station. If he didn't like you, he fired you on the spot. His name was Al Flannigan, but he had earned an appropriate nickname: the Hatchet Man.

Mr. Flannigan and I did not get off to a good start. For my *Wednesday's Child* shoots, I would take extra clothes that were appropriate for the story, such as khaki slacks or walking shorts—business casual for our visits to the zoo or the lake. Then for the newscast, out came the suit and heels. But almost immediately after

Mr. Flannigan took over, a memo went out: *Women are not allowed to wear shorts.* He didn't care what the story was.

My shorts had inspired a station-wide memo.

Why couldn't he simply have told me? I began to feel very insecure around him, especially when I was on the air and knew he was watching. During the newscast, he would sit in the control room with a pad and pen, taking notes of things he didn't like. Well, I was one of those things.

You know how you feel when you just know someone's out to get you? His passive-aggressive scrutiny seemed only to make me perform worse. Fear set in.

One evening after a newscast, I followed Mr. Flannigan out to his Lincoln Town Car limo. I felt as if I had to apologize because I had stumbled over a word while on the air. "Mr. Flannigan," I called out.

He stopped and turned, regarding me with coldness. I pressed on. "I'm so sorry, I just had a bad news day."

He regarded me for a moment, then said, "Do you know what you do? You smack your lips every time you open your mouth."

I was taken aback. "What do you mean?"

He mimicked it by smacking his lips. "You do this—every time."

"I...I'll try to work on that," I replied lamely.

He nodded curtly. "And don't move your eyebrows when you talk. They're too pronounced." Then he stepped into his limo and drove away.

After some time, it became apparent that I just couldn't please him. In fact, the Hatchet Man thought the *weekend* anchorwoman would look better alongside the 6:00 p.m. anchorman—better than me, that is.

"I like her blonde hair better than your short brown hair," he told me bluntly. He told me that I looked too much like anchorman John Pruitt, and that a blonde would match him better. So he pulled me from my position in primetime, which I'd earned by promotion.

I was devastated. I had been down a long road and had taken many twists and turns to get where I was, and now someone else got my job because she had blonde hair? Welcome to the TV news industry, where image is everything.

I went to the news director, who was in my court, and asked what to do about being demoted to weekends. I'll never forget his answer: "Beth, just weather the storm. Flannigan is temporary, and when he leaves, you'll be reinstated on the 6:00 p.m. newscast."

In my mind, however, I was disappointed for the last time with this industry. How could I trust what management said anymore? Once again, it felt as though perhaps I wasn't cut out for the news business.

I had left Tulsa in shame, in pain, running toward a new life where no one knew me. Seeking to reinvent myself in Atlanta, I'd had the chance to heal after the Tulsa experience, but now the Hatchet Man had given me the ax (or so it felt), and I felt all alone.

There was something else, too. That illusion of the white picket fence and what it stood for—home, family, love—was calling me. I had unfinished business in Tulsa: Milton was still in my life and had visited me in Atlanta many times. One day as we were talking over the phone, he said, "Why don't you just come back home to Tulsa?"

I thought, *You know, I think I will.*

The climate in upper management had become more and more disheartening. I made the tough decision to turn in my resignation, pack up my things, and let the excitement of moving back to Tulsa sink in. I returned to the city and the man I loved, to give it another try. I didn't even look for a job. Instead, Milton and I got married.

A couple of months later, I was pregnant.

Motherhood

Love took me back to Tulsa, and love was born to me there: my daughter, Ana Serena. She became my world—the most wonderful thing that's ever happened to me. I had no idea that anyone could love another human being like I loved my baby girl. If I couldn't find success as a career woman, maybe I would find it as a family woman—a wife and mother.

Ana was always an outgoing, smart, and pretty little girl. As a child, she was the tallest in her class and always curious. After a long day at work, when I came home between newscasts, she would meet me at the door. When I would kneel down in my suit and heels and wrap my arms around her little ribcage, it made all my worries of the day subside.

Seeing how much my parents loved their only granddaughter gave me a sense of peace I hadn't felt before. My father taught my little girl how to beat anyone at gin rummy or checkers. He also taught her how to tell jokes and entertain people, and she would use what he taught her to defuse situations quite naturally. It was amazing to me that, as a little girl, my daughter was already intuitive, with a calm demeanor and a child's astounding insight.

At a very early age, Ana learned how to intervene when tempers flared. When my parents came to visit during the holidays, everything would be jolly until invariably the mood of the gathering would shift. Just like when I was a child, my dad would become argumentative. We all knew it was the alcohol. He tried to have fun and enjoy the celebration, but he would get his feelings hurt over the most innocent comment or the look on someone's face. Ana would hear the escalating tone and take her tiny steps toward Papa, taking his giant mitt of a hand in her little one.

"Papa, let's go play cards," she'd say, but, most often, he would get in the car and leave—despite the little feet, tiny hands, and learned jokes.

Ana was the highlight of my life—and still is—but something inside me knew I wasn't really ready to give up on my career. After just six weeks of being a mom, I got a call from KJRH—the Tulsa NBC affiliate. The general manager asked if I was interested in getting back into the business, in returning to the airwaves in Tulsa. I told them that I couldn't—I'd just had a baby!

"When would you consider it?" the GM insisted.

"Maybe in a year," I responded without a moment's hesitation. "Okay, we'll wait," he said. And they did.

They Waited

Eleven months later, I started anchoring the 6:00 p.m. and 10:00 p.m. newscasts on Channel 2.

I was paired up with a great team: dynamic anchor Sam Jones, meteorologist Gary Shore, and sportscaster Jerry Webber. Sam was a hard-core journalist who made a real difference with his documentaries. I can see him now, pounding away at his typewriter, cigarette hanging between his lips, hair always coiffed, and with half a smirk on his face, ready for a joke. Gary, a true scientist, was tall, dark, and quiet. He had his quirky ways, but he brought the level of meteorology to the highest standards of the day. Jerry was probably, in my opinion, the most beloved television professional of all. He was everywhere, every night, with his jeans and boots, navy jacket, white shirt and tie, and great big smile. Jerry eventually transitioned from sports to the anchor chair beside me, which was unheard of in that day. He was so loved by the viewers that it worked. This was the happiest team and TV station I had ever worked for. I was grateful.

I was juggling both sides of myself now: dedicated career woman and loving mother. A huge part of our life was our nanny, Ann Howard, a wonderful, petite, churchgoing source of strength who filled our house with laughter. Ann cared for me as if I were her daughter and Ana as if she were her granddaughter and took us all the way, from changing Ana's diapers to celebrating her graduation from DePaul University. She was a godsend who took care of us for more than fifteen years. We miss her to this day.

And we certainly needed her because my marriage to Milton was deteriorating even before Ana was learning to walk. Sadly, I was learning another major marriage lesson: you might love someone with all your heart, but that doesn't mean you can live with him.

I wasn't in love with my first husband, but he was easy to live with because he was gentle, kind, and even-tempered. The road I had chosen to travel this time was rocky and emotional. After years of therapy, I realized I had married someone like my father, only without the drinking. Milton was handsome and charismatic but could never truly make a commitment. We had been together on and off for years. I had moved back from Atlanta to Tulsa to marry him because I'd wanted to believe that we could be a happy family.

We tried to make the marriage work, but it fell apart in the end. I couldn't take the temper flare-ups or the control factor. I saw it all having an effect on our sweet toddler, who would stretch out her arms in an attempt to stop the yelling. As anyone will tell you, when a child is involved, it changes everything. Plus, I was still needy, and as one therapist told me, "Beth, he'll never give you the kind of support you need."

Ana's father and I were divorced when I was in my midthirties and she was almost three. It was very hard for me to be facing divorce again, but I couldn't possibly regret my attempts to build a family because now I had this precious little girl by my side.

I was disillusioned. I had thought perhaps I could find the success I ached for as the perfect family woman. I'd thought having a baby would make things better. I'd even had a picket fence built. But there was no such thing as the perfect family.

Another one of my illusions was broken.

Fake Red Fingernails

In the mid-1980s, Ana and I lived in a small bungalow in an area of Tulsa called Brookside, several vibrant, tree-filled blocks in midtown. We created wonderful memories of all those important mother-daughter moments, from making chocolate cookies and licking the bowl to playing in the sand at the park. But as a thirty-something single working mom, I was forever torn between my desire to spend every waking moment with my daughter and my need to provide for her and succeed in my career.

After dropping Ana off at elementary school on my way to work at Channel 2, sometimes I would stand at the chain-link fence with my fingers curled around the warm metal bars, staring out over the recess yard. She was playing—so cute! I loved watching her have fun with her friends at school because it was a side I seldom saw. During the hours spent at home with her, we would play together a little, but more often, I would be fixing dinner or checking homework. Gripping that chain-link fence, I could feel my heart sink. I wanted to be on the other side.

Here I was, dressed in my silk suit and high heels, with my bright red fingernails. My eyes went from Ana to some of the mothers who were out there helping in the schoolyard, wearing their shorts, tank tops, and tennis shoes. They looked so comfortable.

Oh, if I could just be there like them! I thought. I envied their casual, comfortable appearance, their freedom to run and play with the kids without worrying about breaking a heel or tearing a fingernail.

What was life like on the other side? What was life like for these moms who didn't worry constantly about meeting other people's expectations? They seemed so confident. Maybe they were so loved at home that other people's opinions didn't matter.

In reality, one of those moms may have pushed back her bangs from her eyes and touched up her ponytail that morning, wishing she had a chance to wash her hair and put on her makeup and really get ready for her day. Maybe she even saw me on the other side of the fence, looking all prepared for a day of work in the newsroom: designer clothes, styled hair, manicured nails. Maybe she thought, *Oh, I wish I had* her *life!*

At times, I wanted to trade in my so-called glamorous life for the freedom to just enjoy my daughter and our time together, to swap my gleaming red manicure for hands covered in white pastry flour, but I've learned it's not fair to judge, and there's no point in envying because sometimes what we think we see may not even be real.

Take these long red fingernails I liked to wear. I looked at them and thought, *How pretty they are!* But they weren't real—they were fake. To some, fake nails may symbolize glamour, luxury, or success. But what do long red fingernails really mean? Do they showcase expensive jewelry or tell the world that you don't do dishes or yard work? Do they suggest sophistication? Professionalism? Money? Perhaps all these things, but those shiny fake red fingernails come with a price.

No matter what they might mean, fake fingernails grow out. The real nails beneath keep growing, and eventually you have to replace the fake ones. You can see the real nail bed between the cuticle and the fake nail. That's not pretty, and it gets worse every day, so the manicured nails need to be either filled in or replaced.

No matter what they might mean, fake nails damage the nail bed—the chemicals eat away at the actual nail and even can seep into the skin. Before they're applied, the real nails must be filed down to a thin layer that becomes weak, bendable, and prone to splits. It takes forever for the real nails to grow back strong.

But with gorgeous, new fake red nails, it's easy not to think about those things. For now, they're pretty. They produce the illusion of prettier, younger, more graceful hands.

I'm not just talking about fingernails now, am I? We do this almost every day of our lives. We create illusions—images of what we think will make us feel better, smarter, richer, prettier, more important. We deceive ourselves and others by producing a false or misleading impression of reality.

What happens when we foster unhealthy expectations or set our sights on false goals—illusions about what it takes to be happy, what success is, or what power is? If you're defining what it means to be happy by what you see on the other side of the fence, you can find yourself trying to climb a ladder of happiness that's leaning against the wrong prop. When you get to the top—if you make it—you may just look around and realize that you've leaned your ladder against the least sturdy thing in your life.

9

Oprah

If you watch your life through the
rearview mirror, you'll get carsick.

—Beth Rengel

Ever since my childhood time spent at my grandmother's house, white picket fences have symbolized for me what home life could or should be: happiness, love, the American dream. Following that dream, I've had picket fences built at all the homes I've owned. In my mind, for a very long time, I really believed that a picket fence meant a happy home. So why was I unable to fulfill the illusion and transform my life into that ideal?

After my divorce from Milton, I swore off men. I concentrated on raising my daughter and working nights for Channel 2. Then some four years later, Don Holloway walked into my life.

He looked like the Marlboro Man. My college roommate from Texas Christian University had insisted we meet, so he flew in from Fort Lauderdale, Florida. He was striking—a tall, tan, blue-eyed pilot. He flew Lear jets and helicopters. Who wouldn't be attracted to him?

We hit it off instantly. He had no children and was eager to move to Tulsa. We dated long-distance for a year, and then he popped the question: "Will you marry me?"

Here it was: another chance at building a happy home. Forever the optimist, I thought, *Maybe this time...*

My Perfect Kitchen

Around the time I met Don, KOTV offered me the opportunity to leave Channel 2 and switch to the Channel 6 affiliate. I was hesitant to make the switch because I had spent five good years with the NBC affiliate, but the offer was very lucrative, and there was no way I could turn it down.

Don had quit his flying job, so now I was the breadwinner. I turned all finances over to him with trust and relief that I had one less thing to do. Ana was six years old and went to a private Catholic school. I got her up in the mornings and got her to school. My day at the office started at 1:00 pm, and I left work after the 6:00 news to go home and fix dinner. The schedule had to be timed perfectly: dinner, check Ana's homework, say prayers, and tuck her in bed and then make a hard, fast drive back to work to do the 10:00 news. It was a full day, five days and nights a week.

Meanwhile, Don tried various jobs, from buying a company that resurfaced bathtubs to selling insurance. It was hard for him to transplant himself from a fast-paced, oceanfront Florida city to my more conventional, landlocked town. He was often called Mr. Rengel, and I'm sure that didn't set well with him. Worst of all, Ana's father and Don seemed to be at war all the time, fighting for control of me and Ana. I saw no way to resolve that relationship.

Don and I bought a house together, and we made our home the focus of our life. That was the one thing he and I had in common. We worked on the old house every weekend for four years, remodeling most of it ourselves. It sat on an acre in the middle of a wonderful neighborhood in midtown Tulsa. Hundred-year-old oak trees were scattered throughout the yard. A flowing creek ran from one end of the yard to the other. Two mallard ducks decided the creek was their home, and there they multiplied to more than a dozen. I fed them each night between the 6:00 and 10:00 p.m. newscasts as though they, too, were part of the family. All I had to do was walk outside to the back patio in my heels and silk suit and call the ducks, and all twelve or thirteen of them would fly to my feet for their dinner. The ducks never left the yard; it was their home—and the home of two rescue dogs, three stray cats, and two white geese I raised. I had a picket fence built along the front yard, naturally, and hand-planted fifty-two rosebushes in front of it.

On the inside, my favorite room was the kitchen—surely the heart and soul of any truly happy home. Don and I rebuilt and decorated the old kitchen with a color scheme of periwinkle blue and buttercup yellow. Many times, we worked past midnight to finish the hand-painted white cabinets and pumpkin-stained beadboard ceiling. I stapled French lace curtains inside the glass cabinet doors. A famous local artist painted the wooden kitchen chandelier, and another artist painted the backsplash tile with a scene from the backyard: the running creek with ducks and all.

All throughout the home, I had placed every accessory in my mind months before the rooms were finished. I had strategically located everything according to my mental image, exactly the way I had seen it in my mind. My illusion of the perfect home, the ideal country kitchen, and the amazing backyard had become a reality.

Better Homes and Gardens magazine thought our house and yard were so impressive, they sent a crew out to photograph it. The crew spent more than eight hours in my house with blazing lights and fresh flowers everywhere, taking hundreds of photos. To think that our home merited that compliment, that it might have its place in a national publication—it was such an honor.

Fast-forward a year to 1996. Walking by the magazine stand at a popular grocery store one May morning, I stopped in my tracks, took a quick step backward, and did a double-take.

That's my kitchen! That's my kitchen! I screamed on the inside. I thought of sitting with my mother all those years ago, dreaming of the perfect home.

I kept my face calm because, of course, no one should ever know what I was feeling inside. But there it was, my kitchen, on the cover of a national publication, *Country Living,* a special edition of *Better Homes and Gardens.*

The article was a year old. Exactly one year ago, the crew had taken those photos and written that article about my kitchen. That's what magazines do with feature stories. It was a scene out of the recent past.

I picked up the beautiful, glossy magazine and caressed it with pride. I was overcome with a huge jumble of other emotions, too. The cover depicted my creation and my lifelong dream—*home.*

Now I stood there, thumbing through the magazine and looking for the story on this kitchen that had been such a labor of love. I found it. It took my breath away. I looked at the photos of the kitchen, of the backyard with the ducks and the creek, of the front yard with my iconic picket fence and the fifty-two rosebushes I had personally planted. The grocery store dropped away, and I was transported a year back in time to what had been, to what was gone now.

I realized this with a growing sadness. Every inch of that kitchen I had created and loved was no longer there. In just a single year, the house had been sold, the kitchen gutted, the ducks and geese removed, and the creek undammed. The new owners didn't like the picket fence, so they tore it down. The fifty-two rosebushes were dug up. It was all gone. Even Don was no longer in my life by that time.

It had been simply another illusion.

Standing there in the grocery store, holding the magazine close to my chest, I clawed my way out of that time warp. I didn't know how to feel: great pride for a job well done? Grief and anguish about what had been and now was no longer? What should I do with all these feelings? I couldn't bring any of it back—the kitchen, the backyard, the picket fence, the husband. The dream was gone.

Eventually, the tidal wave of mixed emotions washed over me, and it left me simply feeling sad and lost, thinking about the ironies of life, but I also felt strangely enlightened.

How many women around the country were thumbing through this same magazine at this very moment, wishing they had what I'd had? How many of them were feeling "less than" because they didn't have a beautiful kitchen like that? Meanwhile, that kitchen didn't even exist anymore, and that illusion of the perfect home— inhabited by a perfect, loving family, naturally—was anything but. Those women were envying what didn't even exist. It was merely a figment of their imaginations and mine, the shadow of a dream I'd once had.

Words from a Wise Woman

Though my four-year marriage to Don was crumbling, my career with KOTV flourished during that time. One of the highlights was being sent to Chicago with my colleague Terry Hood and our photographer, Joe Durant, in the early 1990s. We were there to interview Oprah Winfrey.

Oprah glided through the big double doors of Harpo Studios as if she were walking on air. As she approached, the vibrations in the room immediately changed, and things felt different. It was electric.

Her entourage of some eight employees surrounded her like a flock of geese flying V-shaped high in the sky, following their leader. Her hairdresser, makeup artist, producer, writers—together, they radiated great respect and created a protective cushion around her.

By this point in my career, I had seen many public figures and done many interviews, yet my heart was pounding with awe. I tried to appear cool, though I felt I was standing before royalty. Oprah Winfrey! I was and still am a huge fan.

We were gauged for lights and had microphones clipped to our jackets. Oprah was so gracious, exuding power and confidence even as she made everyone feel comfortable.

"Fabulous suit!" she exclaimed, smiling at me.

Without missing a beat, I said quickly and with pride, "Stein Mart." It was true. I was always happy to find a bargain, and Stein Mart was my favorite discount department store, but now I was silently screaming inside, *What? Couldn't you think of something a little more avant-garde?*

Then Oprah's makeup artist asked, "What eye shadow are you wearing?"

Once again, without thinking, I blurted out, "Max Factor. It's from the drug store." *Oh my gosh!* I thought. *I should have said Chanel.*

I noticed Oprah was wearing gorgeous large diamond earrings and a beautiful ankle-length brown sweater dress, yet near her hip was a little hole the size of a pea—probably a snag that just got bigger, as snags do. I leaned in toward her producer and asked, "Does she know there's a hole in her dress?"

The producer looked at me and replied, "That's a Norma Kamali dress. It's worth about three thousand dollars. It doesn't matter."

Yet I noticed that her fingernails were almost down to the quick. No fake red fingernails for this highly respected and beloved celebrity. Oprah, a nail biter? Suddenly, I admired her even more. She was real, genuine, nice—not to mention brilliant. This billionaire whose image was projected into practically every household in the nation didn't obsess over a perfect image. She didn't live by the illusion.

So there I sat, across from one of the most powerful women in the world. Oprah had single-handedly changed the canvas of the talk show host. She was about to launch her website, which ultimately would bring the world to her. She was an author, actress, producer, philanthropist, and entrepreneur, and she had the most successful talk show in history—just to name a few of her accomplishments.

"Rolling," said Joe, the photographer, pointing for us to "go."

The interview began. Oprah talked about how successful the show had been worldwide but also about the headaches with starting up her new website. She talked about the pressures of having so many employees she cared about and of knowing she was responsible for them.

Then the question was asked, "Are you happy?"

Oprah's reply amazed me: "What is happy? I think that's an overrated word. When I'm out on the farm with my animals, with my God in nature, I feel joy. Yes, I can afford anything I want. I'll never have to worry about money again. But it's the feeling of joy that matters."

The interview lasted about thirty minutes. As we were wrapping up, Oprah asked me, "How about you? What's going on with you?" Her simple yet candid question caught me totally off guard.

At the time, I was going through the terrible breakup with Don. I didn't know what to say other than the truth: "I'm going through a divorce."

"Why?" Oprah asked.

"Well, he doesn't get along with my little girl," I replied. That was the tip of the iceberg, but I was embarrassed to go any further because I sensed I was going to get emotional.

Oprah just nodded. "My best friend, Gail, went through the same thing. Sometimes you don't have a choice, and you do what's best for your child."

Then Oprah stood up, we all shook hands, and we said our thank-yous and good-byes. She walked slowly back toward the same double doors she'd come through with the same V-shaped following of loyal employees. I just watched, feeling humbled that she cared enough to ask me how I was doing. She had almost reached the doors when she said with her billowing voice, without even turning around.

"Remember, Beth, you're doing the right thing. Don't doubt yourself!"

The tears welled up in my eyes. Then Oprah and her entourage walked through the doors, which slammed shut behind them.

Standing there, my mind was blank. I just couldn't move. A tiny feeling of peace grew larger inside me. All those doubts in my heart and mind were quieted just a little bit. The shame and embarrassment that were so much in the forefront with me subsided a bit. I guess I needed someone to say that to me, to validate what I had to do. I know there are two sides to every story, and Oprah had only a glimpse of mine, but it counted.

Oprah's message has always been to find your authentic self. She was one of the world's first acclaimed women to let the cameras see her in gym clothes and without a lick of makeup on. She appeared as a real person, even as she continually tried to keep her weight down. She started a trend among movie stars of saying to the world, "Here I am, like it or not!"

I will cherish that Oprah moment. It started me down the road to understanding myself and the true meaning of home. Is a three-thousand-foot-square house on an idyllic acre what truly moves our hearts? Or are we all just looking for a safe and loving place to land when we fall?

10

Domestic Violence

There is no greater agony than bearing
an untold story inside you.

—Maya Angelou

My marriage to Don had collapsed, and my dream of home along
with it. I knew it wasn't easy being married to me—I had a demand-
ing job that was very public and a grueling schedule that came with
a price—but I couldn't compromise my daughter or myself. After
we decided to call it quits, Don asked for half of my pension and
savings. The case went before a judge, who decided he was legally
entitled to it because we'd acquired a lot of money through my job
while we were married. I appealed, however, and won the battle.
Don went back to Florida, and I had to sell our beautiful home that
was now just a bitter memory.

After my third divorce, still working at Channel 6, I gathered
up my daughter, two dogs, and cat, and rented a ranch-style home
that allowed pets. I put my huge collection of Santa Clauses and
Christmas decorations in the den, which could be cordoned off.
The house foundation had settled so much that not a single bedroom or bathroom door would shut, but still it was home—our
home, Ana's and mine.

After our lease was up, I bought a two-story brick home in midtown, and, yes, I had a picket fence built along the front sidewalk to the front door.

A couple of years went by. I didn't date anymore. My track record was appalling. I didn't trust my judgment on anything other than my work and trying to be a good mother.

Then when Ana was in middle school, one of my best longtime friends introduced me to the man who would become my fourth and last husband. Yes, I fell for the illusion of a happy marriage—again! More than two decades earlier, every night on stage with the New Christy Minstrels, I'd sung the torch song "Maybe This Time." Throughout the years that followed, it seemed to have become my theme song.

My last husband was charming, fun, and funny. He taught me how to play tennis, and I adored his family. We had both gone through counseling to ensure our marriage was the right decision. When it came to marriage, I had always made the commitment with good intentions, certain I could make it work. Never in my mind was there any other reason: for spite, money, revenge, or fear of being alone. This time, I was more determined than ever to learn from my mistakes and make the marriage work. I was so committed, I quit my twenty-one-year career and once again set about creating the illusion of the perfect home.

We lived in a Georgian mansion built in the early 1900s. I restored it to its original beauty, pulling up carpet and tearing off wallpaper and fabric wall covering from the 1970s. It was a labor of joy. I built an exotic koi pond and, around it, my picket fence. Our home became my sanctuary. I didn't miss the television schedule and spent many evenings lingering at dusk with a glass of wine. That first year of marriage, I cooked, played tennis, and traveled with my husband.

But tension was growing between him and my daughter, and it spread faster than the Ebola virus. His temper and his lack of courtesy with my family, friends, and anyone who got in his way were worrisome. My daughter had become a rebellious teenager and, having witnessed the failure of my previous marriage, was already protective of me. She wasn't going to open up to anyone who was so closed off to her.

Within the year, Ana and her new stepfather wouldn't be in the same room with each other. Once again, I watched the relentless and growing disdain between my daughter and my husband manifest into something I couldn't stop. He called her terrible names, and at age fourteen, Ana felt she had no choice but to move out.

That was the beginning of the end of my fourth marriage, but something even more shocking and worrisome put the nail in the coffin.

My charming husband was not always so charming. He'd become more and more verbally abusive and was even physically rough with me at times. One Friday night after being out with friends, he started an argument. He followed me into the kitchen, leaning over me and pointing his finger in my face.

He has totally flipped out this time. I thought.

Then he called me the worst name you can call a woman.

I popped him on the cheek, a quick slap that was unnatural to me. It was a reflex, a response to the angry, hateful word he'd just said about me.

Next thing I knew, I was on the floor. My husband had back-handed me in the face—hard.

I pulled myself up into a sitting position, already crying. It had hurt—both my cheek and my feelings—and I was frightened because this had come from someone I loved in a home I had pretended was happy. Suddenly, I realized I had been in total denial, all too willing to believe my own illusion of the happy home.

He had pushed and shoved me before, but this was the first time he had hit me, and it would be the last. My life changed in an instant. I knew right then that this was it—the marriage was over.

As I've often said in the years since then, I've had coffee breaks that lasted longer. My daughter had moved out, and now I was alone in this giant house with him, but not for long.

Until that moment, I had never experienced domestic violence. *I'm not a victim,* I told myself over and over as he retreated upstairs to the bedroom, cursing with anger. After all, I was the one who reported about this kind of thing happening—*to other people.*

I knew what I had to do. I got up and dialed 911. Then I called my mother and sister, who got to my house just as two police cars arrived, lights flashing.

Two officers went upstairs and knocked on the bedroom door.

"Officer, she faked the fall," I heard my husband say. The police officer downstairs handed me his card and warned me that this incident would probably happen again—only it would be worse next time. He emphasized that if there were any bruises or visible signs of violence, I would have to report it.

My sister took me to the Domestic Violence Intervention Services office to file the report. I felt sure that people recognized my face from television and were looking at us as if I were escorting my sister instead of the other way around. I imagined what they must be thinking: *But that's Beth Rengel from the news. She always seemed so poised and polished. She was in the Miss America Pageant. Surely she doesn't have an unhappy home life.*

The truth is, women who face domestic violence are all around us in this country. Statistics from a Salvation Army report inform us that one out of six women are victims of some kind of abuse. The National Network to End Domestic Violence reports that three women in this country die every day from domestic violence. Men can be victims of violence too, but the overwhelming numbers are adult women. Not only is domestic violence appallingly common, but it is also followed up with questions such as "Why did she stay with him?" There are many misconceptions about how abusive relationships work. Presuming that it's the woman's choice to stay is just another illusion.

Another misconception is that abuse can only be physical. My mother and sister both were victims of verbal abuse, which is just as devastating, except that the bruises are embedded in the soul rather than the body. Both physical and verbal abuse have a direct correlation to a woman's sense of worth.

I had already quit my career. Now I left the big mansion behind, taking just some of the furniture with me. I didn't fight for much of anything financially and even left without a car. My goals now were to heal myself and to restore my daughter's trust in me. I had to show her you can't buy love. I needed to encourage her to see her own worth.

I bought a little house, and Ana moved back home with me. We went back to basics. I needed time to figure out how and why I had been anchored in all the illusions of life. It was a time for healing.

I subscribed to basic cable only, mowed my own lawn, and never put on fake red fingernails again. And I never built another picket fence. I'm not saying it was easy. It was a hard financial adjustment, and it was difficult to overcome another feeling of failure. In hindsight, though, it was the most empowering time of my life. I was myself, and I wasn't afraid of letting anyone down ever again. It was time to strip away another layer of illusion. I wasn't going to give up or give in. It was time to get back up and reinvent myself.

11

The Man Who Taught Me How to See

If we had no mirrors, how content would we be?
If we had no calendar, how young would we feel?

—Beth Rengel

What exactly is illusion? I think it's everything that can be replaced: our cars, our homes, our clothes, our jobs. These are all part of an image we portray to the world.

They're status symbols meant to tell everyone, *I'm rich* or *I'm important* or *I'm loved.*

But who I was—who I am—is not defined by whether my wardrobe was designer or homemade, whether my job was being an anchorwoman or a homemaker, whether my home had a white picket fence or a repossessed sofa. Looking back, I can see that my sister and I were overachievers, as though we felt compelled to live up to a certain image of who we should be. Elaine toured Europe as an opera singer. I just kept reinventing myself. We both made the decision at an early age to never give up, but that also meant never stepping outside that image of perfection or giving ourselves a moment to reflect on who we truly were inside.

If illusion is everything that can be replaced, then what is real? Those things that cannot be replaced: our health, our family, our memories, our dreams. I spent nearly half a lifetime chasing the image of perfection. But as our looks fade, our income changes, or our family moves away, it's what's in our heart that carries us through each day.

I had developed an image based on trying to be perfect and then lived my entire life without stopping to look truly and deeply behind that image. But that was all about to change.

In Jim's Presence

When I met Jim Stovall, it was a delicate and crucial time in my life. I didn't know how far I would go, how deep I could get behind that perfect image, but already I was determined to recover myself and to see what I was truly made of.

I didn't have a clue where to start.

My daughter was about to leave for college. The most important moment in my life had been giving birth to her, and since then, she had been down the rocky road of life with me every step of the way. Watching her grow up to be a beautiful, smart, and caring woman was a joy only a mother can understand. Yet now she was moving onto her own path in life.

The title of news anchor, which had cemented my identity, was gone, too. In the news industry, as on the pageant circuit, my job had depended on a performance, a facade—on chasing down and copying someone else's idea of perfection. Without all that, who was I?

Plus, I was divorced—again.

Without my role as a mother, a career woman, or a wife to fall back on, I was struggling with my ego and self-esteem. Once more I was at a defining crossroads in my life.

In the summer of 2001, I decided, along with two professional friends—an entrepreneur and the owner of a top modeling agency—to conduct a one-time seminar for teenage girls on basic manners. We believed it was possible to build confidence and purpose for young women through developing poise and dignified behavior. This isn't taught in schools today, and many young girls just do not have the benefit of a mother who can teach them how to put their best foot forward. Our goal was to teach everything from using table manners to stepping out of a car gracefully.

One of my colleagues set up an appointment with a public speaker named Jim Stovall, who agreed to meet and give us a quick primer on presentation as we prepared for our seminar. I had never met Jim before, and after hearing his long list of accomplishments, I was awestruck. Jim is a nationally acclaimed speaker and author of more than thirty books, several of which have been turned into movies. He grew up in Tulsa and had been a national champion Olympic weightlifter, a successful investment broker, and an entrepreneur. He is the cofounder and president of the Emmy Award–winning Narrative Television Network, which makes movies come to life for the millions of people nationwide who are blind or visually impaired.

All my life I'd been onstage—from being part of the Miss America Pageant to touring with a musical group to anchoring the nightly news. I knew how to perform. But Jim is on another level entirely. For many, his level of public speaking and the messages he shares are life-changing.

Jim stood up when we walked into the room, and I saw a handsome man in his midforties with a six-foot, five-inch frame and a large build. His rich, deep voice and personality were equally charismatic. I was impressed with him and grateful for his time. After our meeting, I called his office to convey my thanks. To my surprise, the secretary put me right through to him.

"It was my pleasure," he responded. "Want to do it again?"

"Of course!" I replied.

"Well, how about tomorrow at ten o'clock in my office?"

The next morning I got up as usual with my cup of coffee, enjoying the back porch while feeding the birds. As usual, I pondered, *What should I wear?* and *I hope I have a good hair day.* Then I held the cup to my lips and realized it didn't matter.

Jim is blind.

Jim was diagnosed with macular degenerative disease at age 18. He went totally blind at the age of twenty-nine. Still, I wanted to look my best—a long-ingrained habit of mine. So I marched right into Jim's office with a happy, confident attitude—designer suit, poufy hair, bleached white teeth, and all.

After about five minutes of chitchat, Jim leaned back into his brown leather chair, folded his arms, and asked, "Well, what does Beth Rengel want to do with the rest of her life?"

I opened my mouth to say something. Instead, I heard my voice crack. Suddenly, I couldn't keep back the tears. Jim had asked the question of the hour—the question of my life.

Jim handed me a box of tissues, and I told this stranger all my very personal issues. I gushed about the impact of everything from the pageant world to my father issues. I told him about my failed marriages and expressed the difficulties of not living up to other people's expectations. I told him of my public humiliation over getting fired and how I felt as though the entire city of Tulsa had watched my life unfold in a fishbowl: hired, fired, married, pregnant, divorced, hired again, married again, quit a career, and then another divorce to escape abuse.

I finally got control of myself and managed to apologize for my ridiculous honesty.

"It's okay," Jim assured me. "You know, just think about it—I think you need to write a book."

Me? I thought. "But I don't have a story," I protested.

"Yes, you do," Jim replied, smiling gently. "It's a story about getting knocked down and getting back up."

We talked a little more before I drove home, my hands gripping the steering wheel, thinking, *What in the world just happened?*

I slowly realized that for the first time, I had sat in front of someone without being able to hide behind my facade—the illusion of Beth Rengel. My hair, my clothes, my nails, my jewelry, my familiar TV face—it all meant nothing to him. Because he wasn't distracted by what his eyes couldn't see, Jim Stovall had looked right into me. He had listened to my voice and seen my heart.

It left me feeling strangely vulnerable. I realized I'd been hiding behind a mask—a facade that I wanted others to see. Perhaps we all put on that mask to make ourselves appear confident and capable. We hide behind our titles—we're news anchors or teachers, lawyers or mothers, models or social workers. We hide behind the brands of our clothes, the cars we choose to drive, or the neighborhoods we live in. It's all about who we want people to think we are. *This* is the illusion. And trying to keep up with it is like running on a hamster wheel—forever.

Am I really that shallow? I wondered. All my life, it's been about appearance and image, but I hadn't been brought up that way. My family never focused on or cared particularly about such things. What had happened to me along the way?

Deep in Thought

When I was younger, I struggled to be better than I thought I was. Like a lot of teenagers—perhaps girls, especially—I thought that if I could be perfect, I'd be happy and everyone would like me. It was a terrible illusion to try to live up to, and it was only fueled by a pageant system that promoted a single idea of perfection and judged women against those standards—considering, for example, whether a woman's calves meet when she turns her back to the audience.

In truth, no one is perfect—not even Miss America—just as no job is perfect and no relationship is perfect. Yet if we're not careful, we can find ourselves struggling to achieve someone else's idea of perfection for many years. And if you don't fit that image, watch out!

If you're basing your worth on what others think, you are handing over the power to someone else, and that will destroy you in the end. That's what I had done: handed the power to others by trying to live up to the image I thought they wanted to see. My younger self had no self-confidence, and instead of outgrowing this stage and graduating into a more confident adulthood, I went from the pageant race to a profession driven by the same thing: the illusion of perfection. I'd simply traded pageant judges, who all sought the same type of perfection, for news directors, each of whom had a different idea about the ideal woman.

Perfection became a moving target once I'd entered the broadcast business.

Over the course of my career, I worked for five stations in Baton Rouge, Tulsa, and Atlanta. Each station, station owner, and news director had a way they wanted me to be. Like all anchors, I had to prove myself over and over again. Management would change, and so would the idea of who I should be.

I found myself working hard to show a news director what kind of work I put out, to demonstrate the quality of my stories, and to prove my consistency by putting in long days covering elections or a police standoff, late-night football, and weekend parades—and then discovering it was all for naught because that news director only cared about how I looked on camera. Or because that news director was out the revolving door and another was just walking in.

Even after I got out of the business, that thought pattern—*how can I portray the image of perfection?*—lingered with me. After all, it's what I'd known all my life.

Maybe Jim was right. Maybe I did have a story to tell after all.

I began to rethink how I saw myself and others. I realized that this pain that had come from putting so much importance on image was now giving way to a little bit of wisdom: who I am on the inside is quite different from the image I've been projecting to others, and surely that is true for others, too.

Bullies and Red Flags

As a child, when I had disobeyed or behaved badly, my parents knew how to get to me: my punishment was to do yard work. As an adult, I've always adored being in the garden and feeling my hands in the soil. But as a teenager, I hated yard work with a passion. It was hard to look cute while pulling weeds, and in my mind, I had to look cute. So instead of dressing for the chore, I would be kneeling in the flower beds trying to look like Elly May Clampett from the 1960s TV show *The Beverly Hillbillies*. After all, you never know who might be driving by.

Did that make me crazy? Or did that simply make me an insecure teenager who didn't want to give any more ammunition to my schoolmates, the tyrants and tormentors who always seemed to be looking for someone different to pick on?

My own bully, starting in the fifth grade in Brownsville, Texas, was named Cecilia. She had a group of girls who followed her every move and word. At recess, they would come over to me and make fun of my clothes—my homemade clothes. The snickering and laughing made me want to cry. That sense of being judged and those feelings of insecurity only magnified in high school.

I don't think bullies are found only on elementary school playgrounds or in high school hallways. There are adult bullies: husbands, boyfriends, in-laws, not to mention colleagues—in my case, television consultants and news directors—who are paid to criticize and try to make you conform to their image of who you should be. When I was growing up, my mother's attitude was to "kill 'em with kindness," so that's what we did. We pasted on a big grin and said, "Have a nice day!" Only as I got older did I realize that is not valid advice every time for everyone.

Through the years, I have realized that bullies come in all shapes, colors, sizes, and genders. As an adult, I have had a number of encounters with grown-up women who act like bullies. You know who I mean: the women who talk down to you, give you the up-and-down or the once-over, and try to make you feel like a lesser person. But bullies have an impossible image they are trying desperately to live up to, too. Their behavior usually comes from deep-seated insecurities. Intimidating others makes them feel powerful.

Sometimes even professional colleagues, like the person you're sitting next to on set, aren't supportive. I have worked with many coanchors, both men and women, some who had my back and some who wanted to stab me in the back. Some scrambled to have the last spoken word while signing off, even if it was just "good night," because this is seen as portraying power.

Sitting next to the same person five nights a week should create a bond. When you're on the air with your team, sometimes you can sense your partner squirm, and you, too, break out in a sweat. On those wrenching nights, one of us might write a note to the other newscaster, suggesting a question for the interviewee, and pass it discreetly across the desk. That's teamwork—the opposite of bullying.

On the other end of the spectrum, I had one anchorman twirl my chair down several inches before each newscast so he appeared taller and more powerful. When I caught on to what that bully was up to, I began carrying the Yellow Pages with me to the set every night and placing my behind on it to fix that problem.

Another memorable attempt to bully me occurred just thirty minutes before the 6:00 p.m. newscast one evening—the premier of a new news team. It's always important to make a good first impression on the TV viewers, so we needed to look like admiring, supportive partners whose cohesiveness was apparent, but as we finished gathering our scripts to head to the studio, my new coanchor (who was always trying to get rid of his coanchor for some reason or another) rolled his desk chair over to me and looked me squarely in the eyes. "You know, Rengel," he stated, "I'd really rather anchor alone."

As he delivered this swipe of pure intimidation, my head started swimming with questions: *How could he say that? Why would he say that? What happened to putting up a show of support?*

My divine intervention kicked in very quickly. I watched closely as his pupils got bigger, then leaned in to his face and said sternly, "Me, too." I must have made my point because I outlasted all the others, and I was his last co-anchor before he retired.

Facing people who want to judge and belittle is common when you are an on-air personality. Viewers notice everything. One lady told me she couldn't watch the news because of my hairdo. Another viewer called in asking why I wasn't wearing a wedding ring.

More than a decade after that horrible night in 1980 when I accidentally cursed on the air, when I was the newscaster at KOTV, the CBS affiliate in Tulsa, I wore a very small gold cross necklace that was a gift from my sister. After a newscast one evening, I received a phone call in the newsroom from a stranger.

"I notice you're wearing a cross," she said.

"Yes," I replied.

I was surprised she could see it—it was so tiny, you would really have to look closely to see what it was. "My sister gave it to me," I explained.

"Does this mean you won't be cursing on the air anymore?" the caller asked acidly.

I was astounded, but I managed to keep my cool. "You know who you're talking to," I responded, "but I don't know who I'm talking to."

The woman quickly hung up.

There will always be someone who wants to hold your past against you, even after you've cut away your illusions and tried to move beyond your setbacks. We are trained, consciously and subconsciously, to care about other people and their opinions. My first marriage is an example. On my wedding day, I listened to my parents and even my neighbors instead of my inner voice as it screamed, *Don't do it!*

I shushed it up and did what I was supposed to do. I didn't have enough self-confidence to hear that inner voice, so I filled the void with other people's opinions about what was best for me.

When you ignore your inner voice, it eats away at you over time until you feel hollow, like a vessel for the opinions and images of others. Instead, we must learn to ask ourselves, *What is illusion?* and *What is real?* You'll find that most things in life can be replaced—and that the things that cannot be replaced are the only things you need.

So many times, I ignored the red flags. Don't we all? We are trained to believe in the illusion of what could or should be, and often we don't have enough self-confidence to hear our inner voice. Instead, we give too much power to other people's opinions about what is best for us. But those nagging thoughts and feelings that tug at our hearts when we just know something is not right—those red flags are guardian angels saying, "Nooo!" They are your inner voice telling you to *run*.

Why do so many of us ignore those thoughts and voices and just continue to hope things will change for the better? Is it because we refuse to believe what we just heard or witnessed?

The images of perfection we create are strong but not impenetrable. We can stop them from ruining our lives simply by being aware of them. I bought a skillet and hung it on the kitchen wall just to remind me not to ignore those red flags.

What's it going to take next time? I ask myself. *To be hit over the head with a frying pan?*

Are our illusions always bad? I don't think so. Sure, we can find ourselves buried in false images we've created, but as I taught in the seminar for young women, being aware of how we seem to others does not have to betray or be at odds with who we truly are. That's why, even though we shouldn't judge a book by its cover, it's still important to dress appropriately for a job interview. The same goes with building our résumé or shaking hands as a greeting or using good posture, anything by which people will judge us. As long as we're aware of the difference between ourselves and our illusions, there's nothing wrong with creating an image of our best possible self, showing others who we want to be and can be.

That day in Jim's office seems like a lifetime ago. It took me a while to finally get the courage to write my story, the one here in your hands. Jim and I have stayed friends, and I am honored to acknowledge his place in my life and in this book. That encounter between us may have had little impact on him, but it changed my life. And who knows which seemingly minor encounter might change your own.

12

The Illusion of the Perfect Life

Just when the caterpillar thought the world
was over, it became a butterfly.

—Traditional proverb

Over the course of more than twenty years as a reporter, I came across some life-altering stories that changed my thinking about what is powerful and what is pretty.

I've had a few moments of epiphany in my own personal life, too. Most of them have to do with the same idea: basing your happiness on appearances is like trying to build castles on a cloud. There is no such thing as a perfect life, and trying to build one will just leave you free-falling from the skies with no parachute.

So illusion is often a bad thing, but it can be a very good one, too. First impressions are powerful, so you've got to put on your best face. We do judge a book by its cover. It has to intrigue us, or we don't pick it up. Let me put it another way:

For those of us who aren't connoisseurs, how do we choose a new bottle of wine? I like the look of some labels and steer clear of others. If it doesn't look interesting, I won't pick it up. Now that I'm in the real estate profession, I tell homeowners that selling their house starts with curb appeal, which will entice a buyer to want to look inside the house. What do we do to invite people in? We spruce up the exterior of the house and make it look pretty.

But life isn't always pretty, and many times you have to look beneath the surface to find out what's really going on and what's really important. That's never been more evident to me than at certain points in my life, which I want to share with you now.

What Truly Matters

The last remaining leprosy colony in the United States used to be located in Carville, Louisiana, about twenty miles from Baton Rouge. The people who lived in Carville were so scarred and deformed from the scourge now known as Hansen's disease that it was very difficult to function in mainstream America. Ravaged by a horrible condition that scientists still don't fully understand, they were banished to facilities like this one and then forgotten. Yet the perspectives I encountered in Carville had a profound impact on me.

While working at WBRZ, I had the opportunity to interview a man who was diagnosed at the age of eighteen while living in San Francisco. No one knew what was wrong with him. He was placed in intensive care as the sores ate away at his body. When the doctors finally figured out it was leprosy, he was shocked. Wasn't this a disease of the past—of biblical times or the Middle Ages?

He volunteered to do an experimental treatment, but it stunted his growth. When I met him, he had no toes and no fingers past the middle knuckle, and his eyes seemed to be bulging out of his head. You might think that a man like this couldn't be happy or feel worthwhile. After all, what sort of life could he have?

But this man, horribly disfigured with Hansen's disease, had built his own ham radio and spent a great deal of time on that radio, talking to truckers. His handle was Trader Joe, and everyone seemed to know him. He made it his business to warn travelers about traffic jams and road conditions. Refineries were everywhere in that industrial part of Louisiana, which meant there was always an explosion or some sort of accident truckers would be better off avoiding. Trader Joe knew about them all, and he kept his radio friends informed.

Not only that, but this man was also an artist. The way he held his paintbrush was phenomenal, and the art he created was nothing short of brilliant. The shocking image he presented physically was such a sharp contrast to the beauty of his work and the important effect he had on people's lives. When I first met him, I found it hard to look at him, yet from his heart, he created these stunning masterpieces.

He also had a girlfriend. She, too, was a victim of leprosy, and seeing them together, I began to glimpse what they really looked like on the inside—a hint of the beauty they saw in each other. This profound proof that beauty really is in the eye of the beholder presented a whole new twist on what pretty is.

I had a similar experience some years later when I spoke with a high school junior from one of the communities surrounding Tulsa. This young man was born with no arms, but he was one of the best students in shop class. He worked the electric saws and used the hand tools—and did it all with his feet!

"How do you get dressed?" I asked him.

He smiled and said simply, "With my feet."

"How do you eat?"

A bigger smile. "With my feet."

He did everything with his feet, and he did it amazingly well. Rather than let this disability control his life, he had developed skills and an amazing attitude to go with it.

At one point, I asked him, "What do you miss?" I thought he might talk about playing sports or video games.

His answer rocked me: "I miss the ability to hug."

This young man could do so much, had mastered so much of his world. He faced his imperfect life with the right attitude, always looking at what he *could* do instead of focusing on what he *couldn't*. And his heart shone through the illusion of physical imperfection. He didn't miss some shallow, temporary thing—he missed being able to share love in that simplest of forms: a hug.

While I wasn't blind to the messages behind these encounters, nor did I put two and two together right away for an understanding of what truly matters in life. I didn't see things quite the same way back then, wrapped up as I was in appearances and the image I'd chosen for myself.

All too often, we create these grand images of what our life should look like—the meaning of success, fulfillment, fun, or love. We think these things must be expensive or out of reach, only to be found traveling across distance and time to some other place far away from here. But oftentimes, what we really need for our "perfect" life exists right in our own backyard. It's the little things we remember—like hugs—that actually bring the most fulfillment.

Through a Child's Eyes

Though they were constantly living under financial stress, my parents afforded the best they could for me and my sister. In my case, I could afford much more in the way of gifts, travel, and other such things for my daughter. As a working mom, I sometimes planned a week out of town so we could pack in all the fun and pleasure we were missing because of my career. When Ana was six years old, I chose Disney World in Florida for our vacation.

Ana and I flew to Orlando and spent the first day at the Magic Kingdom. We saw Mickey Mouse and the other characters, rode the rides, and ate overpriced theme park food. The next day, we visited Epcot Center, enjoying the "world's fair" atmosphere. The third day, we headed to the beach and played all day in the sand. On the remaining days, we indulged ourselves, eating out and shopping to our hearts' content.

On the plane ride home I was basking in the exhausted afterglow of such a busy trip, tallying up the costs in my head. Maybe I needed some validation because I turned to Ana and asked, "Honey, what was your favorite part of the trip?"

She looked up at me and gave an amazing six-year-old answer: "When we tickled on the bed!"

At these sweet, candid words, I swallowed hard, forcing a smile and turning away to look out the window so she wouldn't see the tears welling up. *We could've done that at home, for free,* I thought, *every day of the year.*

Perhaps this view is childlike, but enjoying the little things is a simple path to true happiness. What would happen if we were to reject the mounting illusions and the pressure to go bigger and better, to do more? To a happy and loved child, life is as perfect as it needs to be.

What Ana wanted most, what she dreamed of, was the undivided attention of her busy mom. We found that a thousand miles from home, but we could've found it in our own backyard.

Living by the Clock

Discovering what will make us truly successful, fulfilled, and happy is a lifetime journey. Are our goals in life elaborate and extravagant because those are the goals we've been told we should chase? Or do we seek the kind of simple pleasures that are more real, attainable, and lasting? Our choice may determine whether we spend our lives seeking perfection or decide to recognize the perfection all around us. Perspective makes all the difference.

If you want perspective, try looking back on your calendar. What were you worrying about this time last year? I find this comforting because those things that may have seemed crucial can seem so trivial just a year later.

My whole life used to revolve around the calendar and the clock. When I worked in a newsroom, my eye was always on the clock. Raising a little girl as a single mom and working the evening newscasts, I had to juggle a lot of responsibilities. I had to know exactly what time it was at all times. The gift my daughter wanted most—my time—was the one that was hardest for me to give.

For even greater perspective on how precious time is, spend some time with the elderly.

Time stands still in a nursing home. The residents start coming to the cafeteria early for lunch or dinner because for many of them, it's the highlight of their day. I think if I were in their position, I'd wish there was a chore to do or a deadline to meet. The silence of a nursing home somehow recalls for me the happier sounds of a busy newsroom or kids playing in the backyard.

Not too long ago, while visiting my mother in her nursing home, I couldn't help but overhear a group of senior ladies talking.

"What day is this?" one asked.

Another answered, "I don't know."

I piped up. "It's Thursday."

"Thursday?" one lady said, looking first at me and then away, out the window. "I thought it was Sunday..."

In her early nineties, my mom seldom knows what day it is, what month it is, and needless to say, what time it is. It's not exactly the way we picture the final years of our life, is it? My dad has been gone more than a decade. My sister moved to Kansas City. My daughter moved across the country. It has been left to me to tie up the loose ends of Mom's life. I've had to sell her car, sell her home, and move her into a succession of nursing homes until she outlived her savings and is now in a Medicaid facility. My mother is still here, but in many ways, she's not.

These days, instead of living my life by the clock, I find myself spending more time with my mom at the nursing home, where time stands still. No more long talks over milk and cookies for us. Instead, I'm left wondering, every time I visit, whether it's the last time I'll see her. I miss her wisdom. I knew she had been through a tough life, but she always taught me to do the right thing. Watching her grow older has been a lonely and sad journey, but there have also been blessings. My flexible schedule as a realtor has given me the opportunity to take care of my mom and just spend time with her as she has aged. I've learned not to wish for all those other things we used to have. Life ticks by, and we have to appreciate the little moments, or we'll look back and wish we hadn't wasted them wishing for tomorrows.

When Ana was six years old, my parents moved to Tulsa to be near their only grandchild. Oftentimes, my mother gladly came to the house to babysit. It seemed I was always in a hurry to get back to the newsroom. One night at bedtime, as I prepared to leave for work, my mom got in bed with my little girl because it was easier to get Ana to sleep that way. Pulling the covers up over both of them, I realized I was looking down at the bookends of my life: my mother and my daughter.

I bent down to kiss Ana's cheek. My sweet little girl's hair smelled like clean shampoo, and her skin was warm and smooth. I moved to kiss my mother, whose hair was gray and stiff, whose wrinkled skin was a little cold and clammy. Both looked up and smiled at me as I was about to leave. What a moment.

I was thinking about how, after a long day in heels, I couldn't wait to get home and hug my little girl as she wrapped her arms around my neck. There is nothing to this day that feels so meaningful, especially now that I know those hugs and cuddles don't last forever. That hug from my daughter changed what kind of day it had been for me. Everything melted away, and all was good with the world. Now I live on the memories of such hugs.

"Do you miss hugs?" I asked my mom as she lay in the bed with my daughter.

"Of course I miss hugs," she replied. "Just because my skin is wrinkled and I'm an old woman doesn't mean my insides are any different."

Now that I'm older and my daughter is a mother, I think about that conversation all the time. I get it now. Some things never change, like the need for a hug. What could be more precious?

In My Own Skin

I left newscasting for good in the 1990s. When I went back to work, I decided to change careers and get into real estate. It didn't matter anymore how young or thin I looked. I had a service to give to people, and it came easily because of the love for my adopted hometown, Tulsa. I walked through my fear of change and made it happen.

I walked through another fear in my mind when I picked up boxing. It is an empowering and disciplined sport, and it makes me feel like the fighter I've come to know I am.

I feel more comfortable in my own skin now, and I still live by those three clichés that have driven my life:

I don't regret the things I do, only the things I don't do. I try new things because I'll never know unless I try.

And anyway, if I fail, it's better than a kick in the ass.

With these words, the traditions of my grandmother, my mother, and my father live on.

Life is full of traditions, isn't it? And they seem to become more significant as we age. I started my own tradition—collecting Santa Clauses—when my daughter was born. Christmas was always my favorite time of year. I wanted to believe there was a magical man at the North Pole whose purpose was to make life better for all of us by stopping in to leave a token of sweetness each year.

We still put out cookies and milk even when Ana was in middle school. I used to think I'd trick her by saying, "Now when you stop believing in Santa, that's when he'll stop coming to our house." She probably rolled her eyes and played along with my illusion about Christmas, for my sake.

Over the years, I have acquired many styles of Santa statues: small, tall, Western-style, Old World, contemporary, elaborate. I would begin decorating for Christmas the week before Thanksgiving. It took me that long because I had quite a collection. I love each one of my Santas.

Years ago, I had my eye on one Santa in particular, standing in the aisle of a wonderful holiday store all season long. He was a life-size, Victorian-style Santa with long silver hair, a burgundy corduroy robe, and grapevines coming over his hood and down his sides. He had the kindest, most beautiful ceramic face with little wire-rimmed glasses. But he wasn't cheap. I told myself I wasn't going to buy him unless he went on sale.

So the day after Christmas, I was the first one at the store, with my nose pressed against the glass door. The sales associates all knew what I was after—I had admonished them over and over: "Don't sell him!"

The manager unlocked the door at 10:00 a.m., and I made a beeline back to my Santa Claus. Even heavily discounted, he was still expensive, but I just had to have him. The cost: $1,000, and this was more than twenty-five years ago.

I brought home my prize, and he has been a feature in my home, wherever I have lived. He stands tall alongside the fireplace, with dignity and a joyful, protective demeanor. He has become part of my life. Many Christmases, the holiday would be hollow for me, divided because my daughter would spend half the time with her father, but my tall Santa was always there, comforting.

One particular Yule night, I was sitting in my living room with the fire going. The Christmas music was playing in the background, and I sat in the wingback chair with a glass of Chardonnay, listening to Celine Dion sing "All by Myself."

Here I am, alone again, I thought. But now I knew something I hadn't before: alone is not the same as lonely.

Suddenly, a nagging, overwhelming urge came over me, and I put down my glass of wine and went over to my Santa. I reached out my arms to him and, very carefully, hugged him with great appreciation. Under his robe, the Santa was just a stick frame, but I put both arms around him anyway and thanked him for always being there for me. After all, Santa has been with me longer than any husband. He has never hurt my feelings, never said an unkind word. He's just the strong and silent type. He has watched as all the illusions I surrounded myself with all my life—perfect beauty, perfect marriage, perfect career, perfect family, perfect home— have fallen away one by one. He's still with me, and he doesn't care about perfection.

My life's not perfect, but then again, whose life is?

EPILOGUE

Your heart is your compass.

—Beth Rengel

I know now what is real—the love I've given and received in my life. Everything else was an illusion that I can let go. This I've learned and accepted over many years, many ups and downs, many sorrows, and many joys. Isn't it amazing how each day, with every situation, we are presented with opportunities to learn from our experiences and encounters? Life is a great journey we travel, and we gain wisdom from the choices we make.

This book is my story, from my experiences. Each and every person has a story to tell. The choices we make on a daily basis can affect us not only on that day but for the rest of our lives. That is a powerful gift we have been given.

I am grateful you picked up this book and am honored to have shared some personal moments with you. In the news industry, I wrote news stories, documentaries, and magazine articles, and I got paid to do it. But writing this book was different. It was like having open heart surgery. It's painful, but you know you have to go through it to heal.

I have healed and continue to heal, and I will leave you with these lessons I've learned along the way:

Believe in yourself. You're not your job, your title, your clothes, your car, or anything else you might be hiding behind. Figure out who you truly are. Stand tall and proud. Accept and be faithful to that true self. Don't let anyone tell you who you are. Just be the best possible version of you.

Dare to take risks. Giving in to your fears will leave you wondering what might have been. You'll never look back in regret on the things you dared to try. Reinvention has been a theme of my life. Why not try it in yours?

Find your own song and sing it. Your song comes from your inner voice, and to find it, you'll have to dig. It took me years to hear that voice and even longer to listen to it instead of listening to other people. Turn up the volume from within.

Look for the light inside you. Each one of us is filled with a unique and bright light—I truly believe this. Don't let your light frighten you. Don't ever doubt your worth. You are more loving and powerful than you think you are.

Surround yourself with people who bring you up, not those who tear you down. Appreciate the ones who have helped you in rough times. Be aware of those who have disappeared or, worse, put you in harm's way. There are bullies out there, but you don't need to buy into their illusions. You are stronger than you realize.

Follow your dreams wherever they take you. Discover your passion and stick with it. Never give up your power. Make a contribution. Don't be afraid to stumble and always make the decision to get back up. Most of what we see as failures are only setbacks.

Finally, don't get caught up in the illusions of life. Life isn't always fair. A perfect body, a perfect childhood, a perfect romance, a perfect family—none of these are attainable. They are simply images we try on for size and, if we are wise enough, discard before it's too late. Get beyond these illusions, and you'll see that we are all connected. You'll be free to develop a truer vision of yourself and your life. If your vision is your own, you will own your vision.

And every now and then, let yourself enjoy the pleasure of a Ding Dong.

ABOUT THE AUTHOR

Author and speaker Beth Rengel is a well-known personality with a history in the public eye. Over the course of more than two decades, she had a successful television career as a reporter and evening news anchor in Baton Rouge, Louisiana; Atlanta, Georgia; and Tulsa, Oklahoma. She covered stories such as one of the worst oil spills in the Gulf of Mexico and the 1995 Oklahoma City bombing. She interviewed famous women, from supermodels to first ladies to, her favorite, Oprah Winfrey. Never afraid to get up close and personal with the story, she was one of the few reporters to visit the only facility in the country for people afflicted with leprosy. In 2014, Beth was inducted into the Oklahoma Women in Journalism exhibit as one of the pioneer women in broadcast news.

Driven to succeed even as a young woman, Beth won the title of Miss Texas and came in third at the 1973 Miss America Pageant. She then had the opportunity to tour Europe with the Miss America USO show and to lead the successful folk group New Christy Minstrels as it toured all over the United States.

Beth is a natural communicator who can make you laugh and cry with stories of success and failure. Her love of writing started when she was a girl, though she never thought she would someday use her life experiences to inspire others. Today, she resides in Tulsa with her two rescue dogs and watching her granddaughter, Bella, grow up.

Beth Rengel (Mae Beth Cormany)
5 years old with cat "Toy".

Rider High School
cheerleader in
Wichita Falls, Texas.

Miss Astros - Houston
Baseball Team 1969-1970.

Mae Beth Cormany

MISS TEXAS

My dad and me in my one piece swimsuit that my mom cut in half. 1970

Moments after the crowning on stage at the Miss Texas pageant.

Here She Comes . . .
Lovely Miss Texas

Dallas Morning News magazine cover 1972.

MISS TEXAS

This is a typical Texas Parade with cowboys and horses in the background.

My beautiful sister on stage in Europe as a lyric soprano opera singer.

Here are my parents form Wichita Falls and my sister who flew in from Europe the day after winning the title.

The Evening Gown Competition walk down the runway that
was the length of a football field that felt longer!

Top 10 in Swimsuit competition in Atlantic City with Bert Parks.
This was his last year to emcee the Miss America Pageant.

Top Five in the Miss America Pageant.

A Texas promotional picture for a large department store.

USO tour in Germany.

This is how we traveled with the
USO Tour.... by helicopter.

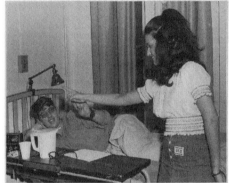

We toured many Veterans Hospitals in Germany while on USO tour.

I took lead singer position of The New Christi Minstrels folk group in 1974 after the former lead singer won Miss America.

Mike Rengel, former NFL New Orleans Saints football player and me on vacation in Jamaica 1974.

Modeling days in
New Orleans.

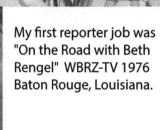

My first reporter job was
"On the Road with Beth
Rengel" WBRZ-TV 1976
Baton Rouge, Louisiana.

143

First evening anchor job at ABC's KTUL "Total 8 Tulsa".

"8's the Place" ABC Tulsa Anchor team, Bob Hower, Chris Lincoln and Don Woods promotional shoot to look like movie stars just getting out of a limousine. My coat was a borrowed rabbit coat.

Another five-star promo by KTUL at the race tracks.

WXIA - TV Atlanta 5:30 p.m. weeknight News Team. Meteorologist Guy Sharp, Anchor Chuck Moore and former football player and sportscaster Harmon Wages.

Tulsa's NBC affiliate evening newsteam meteorologist, Gary Shore, Anchor Jerry Webber and sportscaster Al Jerkins.

With daughter
Ana Berry before
dance recital.

My favorite Christmas picture of my parents.... or not?

Epcot Center and Disney World after spending a lot of money when Ana's most fun were the simple things!

Our wonderful nanny, Ann Howard, Ana and my mom, Serena.

Eighth year of MDA Telethon with Jim Giles and CNN Anchor Bob Losure.

KOTV Anchor Team, Meteorologist Jim Giles, Sportscaster, John Walls and Anchor Clayton Vaughn. We were on a bus tour and did newscasts live on location.

My Kitchen on cover of Better Homes and Gardens Magazine in 1996 that I designed.

Hanging out with
Oprah 1990.

On the set with Oprah!

Daughter, Ana at DePaul University in Chicago.
OU - Texas rivalry.

Mother-Daughter date in New York City!

My mentor, author and speaker, Jim Stovall. 2014

My Santa!

Made in the USA
Columbia, SC
10 June 2017